ERICA WILSON'S
QUILTS OF AMERICA

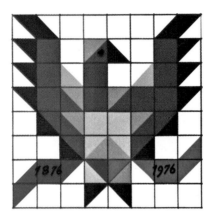

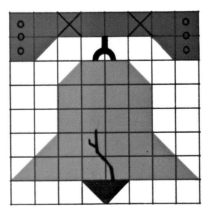

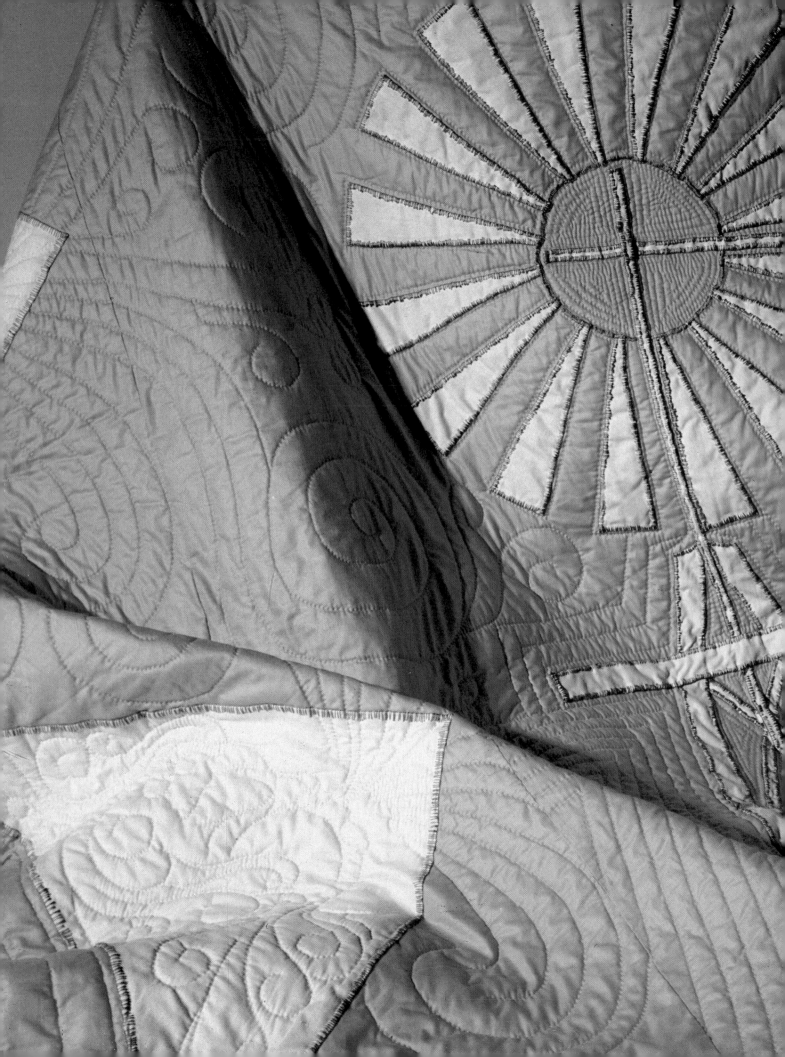

ERICA WILSON'S
QUILTS OF AMERICA

OXMOOR HOUSE, INC. BIRMINGHAM

Copyright© 1979 by Erica Wilson
717 Madison Avenue, New York, New York 10021

Conceived, edited and published by Oxmoor House, Inc.
Book Division of The Progressive Farmer Company
Publisher of *Southern Living*®, *Progressive Farmer*®, and
Decorating & Craft Ideas® magazines.

Eugene Butler	Chairman of the Board
Emory Cunningham	President and Publisher
Vernon Owens, Jr.	Senior Executive Vice President
Don Logan	Vice President and General Manager
Gary McCalla	Editor, *Southern Living*®
John Logue	Editor-in-Chief
Mary Elizabeth Johnson	Senior Editor, Crafts
Candace N. Conard	Editor, Crafts
Mary Jo Sherrill	Associate Editor, Crafts
Jerry Higdon	Production Manager
Mary Jean Haddin	Copy Chief

Erica Wilson's Quilts of America

Editor: Candace N. Conard
Design: Viola Andrycich, Steve Logan
Photography: Robert Perron, Seth Joel, Shecter Lee
Technique Illustrations: Danielle Hayes
Pattern Illustrations: Janette Aiello

Special thanks to Robert Kline of the U.S. Historical
Society; to all at the Smithsonian Institution, espe-
cially Rita Adrasko, Doris Bowman, and Nancy Davis;
to Jean Mailey of the Metropolitan Museum of Art; to
Phyllis Haders and Dr. Bishop of the Museum of
American Folk Art; to Cecelia Toth of *Good Housekeeping*; to Mary Stieglitz of the University of Wisconsin; to my staff; to Viola Andrycich; to my husband
Vladimir Kagan, great photographer and critic; to
Ben Mildwoff; to the quilters—all 10,000 who entered
the Great Quilt Contest; and especially to *Good
Housekeeping* for sharing photographs and some of
the patterns of the winning quilts.

Photographs on pages 49, 59, 62-63, 64, 73, 81, 85,
and 87 were shot on location in the Museum of History and Technology, Smithsonian Institution.

Pages 12-26, 31, 37-38: Excerpts from *The Quilters:
Women and Domestic Art*. Patricia Cooper and
Norma Bradley Buferd, copyright © 1977 by Patricia
Cooper Baker and Norma Bradley Buferd. Reprinted
by permission of Doubleday & Co.

The categorization and paper-folding systems contained on pages 128-129 are from *Patchwork Patterns* copyrighted 1979 by Jinny Beyer, EPM Publications, Inc., McLean, Virginia.

The butterfly quilting patterns on pages 208-209 are
copyrighted by Leman Publications, Inc., Wheatridge,
Colorado, publisher of *Quilters Newsletter* magazine.

Library of Congress Catalog Number: 79-88456
ISBN: 0-8487-0504-1
Manufactured in the United States of America
Seventh Printing 1986

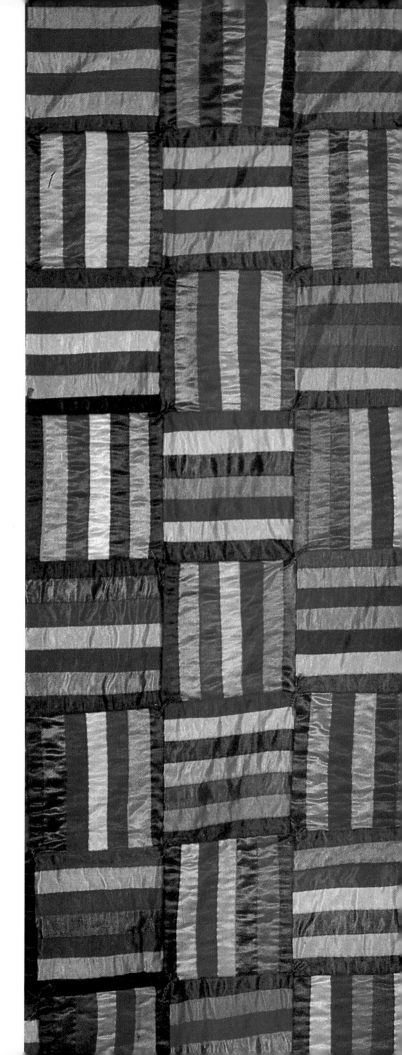

CONTENTS

Silk and satin Rail Fence quilt. Ben Mildwoff collection.

Ray of Light, created by Jinny Beyer from Virginia, was the National Winner in the Great Quilt Contest.

This book is just a short length of the continuous thread forming the story of quilt making in America. No other form of needlework seems to have become so closely involved with the history of this country and with the lives of our people.

The Great Quilt Contest was the brainchild of Robert H. Kline, president of the U.S. Historical Society. In 1975, in cooperation with the Museum of American Folk Art in New York City, he formulated a plan to find the one most outstanding quilt from each of the 50 states plus the District of Columbia. His idea was to organize a contest with the help of a national magazine and exhibit the winners in a book and a travelling show so that they could be enjoyed and appreciated by all.

The U.S. Historical Society, a private, non-governmental organization, might be called a national trust for "things." It works in cooperation with museums and other institutions in reproducing such memorabilia as historic firearms, swords, fine art prints, furniture, stained glass, and other art objects. From time to time, the Society has also sponsored national programs to encourage greater interest in America's heritage.

The Great Quilt Contest prompted 10,000 entries (2000 from California alone), fortunately all in photographic form. Five hundred quilts were selected as runners-up, and from those, fifty-one winners were chosen. Judging the overwhelming number of entries was a dazzling experience. The judges—Doris Bowman, textile curator of the Smithsonian Institution; Phyllis Haders, quilting authority; Jean Mailey, textile curator of the Metropolitan Museum of Art; Cecelia Toth, needlework editor of *Good Housekeeping*; and the author—took weeks to narrow the field from 10,000 to 500. The quilts were judged on overall beauty, with specific attention given to design interpretation, color selection and combination, materials used, quilting technique, general workmanship, and originality.

The Smithsonian Institution Traveling Exhibition Service (SITES) is showing a selected group of winners of the contest, travelling to museums throughout the United States. The exhibition of winners was organized by the U.S. Historical Society with the support of this publisher.

The happy task of preparing the book of the Great Quilt Contest fell to me as a member of the Advisory Committee of the U.S. Historical Society. In contacting many of the contestants by phone and through letters as well as in person, I feel I have come to know them, and I have found there is a story behind every quilt that was entered. Their stories, together with those of quilters in other times, may be found on the following pages. Perhaps by absorbing the ideas of the prizewinning quilts, as well as those of the masterpieces from the past, present and future generations may be inspired to try their hand at this most satisfying and beautiful form of needlework.

The judges of the Great Quilt Contest examining the entries: left to right, Doris Bowman, Phyllis Haders, Jean Mailey, Erica Wilson, and Cecelia Toth.

1

QUILTING IN AMERICA

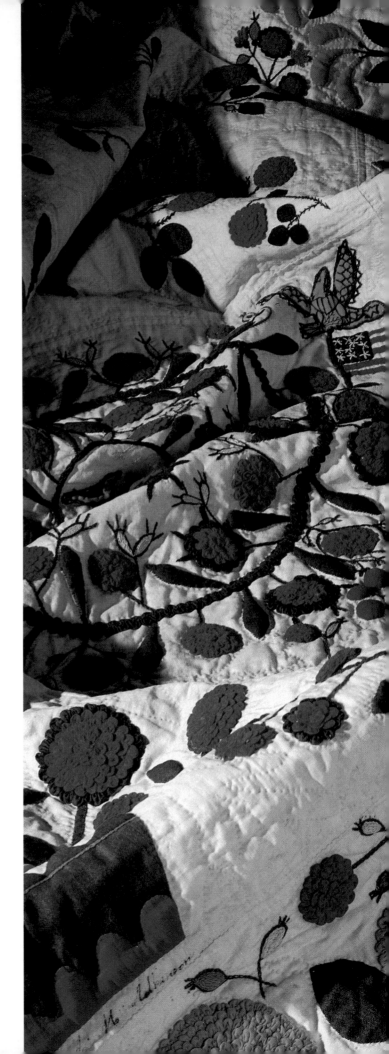

France has petit point, England has smocking, Scandanavia has white openwork embroidery. But patchwork is a needle art that is America's own, and perhaps no other art form so symbolizes the pioneer virtues of thrift, industry, and ingenuity that built America.

For the New England colonists and later for the settlers of America's West, quilting was a necessity, not only because it provided warm bedcovers, insulation against harsh winters, and a means of renewing worn clothing; but also because it acted, in some measure, as solace to the strong women who spent their days struggling to survive. Out of these needs and a scarcity of fabrics, a brilliant art form emerged—patchwork quilts.

In ancient times, the Chinese rarely discarded old clothing because they felt that, through use, the fabrics became part of the wearer. As a result, old fabrics were recycled onto new ones; fragments of old cloth were laid down on new silk fabric, as shown on page 5, and fashioned into what appears now to be a very contemporary design. The edges of the appliquéd material were frayed to soften and blend the two fabrics together, then the "patches" were covered with rows of running stitches for strength and unity.

Like the Chinese, Americans also preserved the memories of those gone before by handing down precious fragments of clothing. Generations of quilters in America passed their knowledge from one to the other like links in a chain, forming an unbroken record of history that continues to this day. The whole fabric of life that went into the building of America was built into the quilt as well with motifs of covered wagons and log cabins, windmills and tumbleweeds. The quilt in America is so much a part

Maryland quilt worked in appliqué, embroidery, and ruching, circa 1850. Smithsonian Institution.

2

of its history that the two are enmeshed together like one precious fabric, embroidered upon from the time this country was born.

Quilting (a sandwich of two layers of fabric with padding between, held together by stitching) was popular in medieval times. Knights went into battle with quilted coats under their

Opposite: One corner of a magnificent sunburst quilt made by Mary Wilcox Taylor in 1850, Detroit, Michigan. Hundreds of diamonds of pieced silk radiate from the central sun, while appliquéd fabric "paintings" of rural scenes, fruits, birds, Fort Dearborn and the American flag, and two hunters and their dog form the border. Smithsonian Institution.

Above: Fragment of an oriental silk appliqué with clouds in yellow, brown, and black on a cream white background, reinforced with running stitches. Japanese eighth century; said to be from the Horuji. 10¾" x 11⅜". Metropolitan Museum of Art (Purchase Rogers Fund, 1944).

armor that acted as "shock absorbers" and with quilted outer garments to prevent their armor from rusting in the rain or absorbing the heat of the sun. Quilted coverlets were popular with the Elizabethans, and the well-dressed English gentleman was often so "stuffed and padded" with quilted jackets and waistcoats that he found it difficult to move.

In America, the magnificent pieced work exemplified by the quilt on page 4 probably began with a single patch. Every scrap of fabric was precious to the pilgrims, who had no cloth available other than what they had brought from Europe or could make by hand, which was a long and difficult task. In fact, it was not unusual for clothing to be patched and

worn for twenty years, then cut down for a child, and finally recycled on a quilt.

Eventually, the colonists' bedcovers, like their clothing, were patched over and over to the point that the original designs were completely hidden under the irregularly shaped scraps of fabric. New quilts were similarly made of patches on a muslin backing, overlapped without any formal design to save on thread and fabric.

None of the earliest American quilts have survived to the present because they were made of fabric already worn thin with age. The informal style of patching was revived in Victorian times when the crazy quilt, shown here, became the fashionable throw for every proper Victorian parlor. But, unlike the drab colored scraps of puritan clothing, Victorian crazy quilts, by comparison, seemed to explode with the colors and textures of exotic materials—silks, satins, brocades—and were covered with whatever decorative stitching struck the quilter's fancy.

Appliqué, the art of stitching one fabric on top of another, was known to the ancient Egyptians, the American Indians, and the accomplished European needlewoman. But for the pre-revolutionary American home, it represented a thrifty way to embellish a bed, which was often the most prized piece of furniture in the house. By the early 1700s, the fine, hand-painted Indian chintz and palampores (printed or painted cotton cloth) were available in America, and by cutting out pieces of this precious material and appliquéing them in pretty arrangements on top of plain muslin, the colonial lady could stretch a single yard of

Left: Detail of a crazy quilt with silk stitching. Ben Mildwoff collection.

Opposite: Nineteenth century crazy quilt in silks, velvets, and brocades with silk embroidery. Author's collection.

6

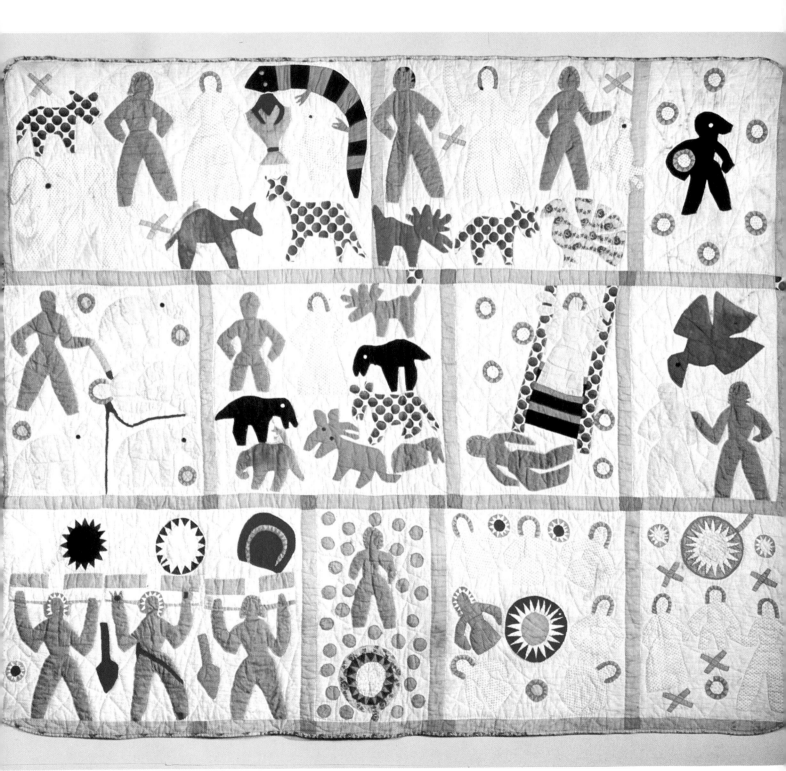

8

expensive fabric to cover an entire quilt.

As with patchwork, appliqué later became an art form in itself as women worked scraps into magnificent pictorial arrangements, added embroidery, and even plumped up their cutout designs with padding, as in the marvelous Garden of Eden quilt shown on pages 10-11, made by Abby Belle Ross in 1874. The creator was obviously a master of appliqué as well as an accomplished artist because the turnbacks are executed so finely that the design almost appears to be painted on the cloth: tiny insects with embroidered legs, spotted giraffes, and Adam rushing ardently towards Eve as she relaxes on a rock.

The scene in which an unwitting Eve is being beguiled by the giant snake is a detail from another masterful Garden of Eden quilt, worked in the late 1800s. The quilter included scenes from the Fall from Grace around a central sun and moon, representing a glorious "firmament," and encircled the entire work with two branches of the Tree of Life.

The religious theme was a common one in pioneer America, and probably the most noted religious needle artist was a black woman named Harriet Powers. Mrs. Powers was a Georgia farm woman who worked two quilts in the late nineteenth century by stitching together blocks of scenes from the Bible, from

Opposite: Harriet Powers Bible quilt made in 1886, Georgia. Smithsonian Institution.

Above: Detail of Garden of Eden quilt worked in the late 1800s. Smithsonian Institution.

the Garden of Eden to the Crucifixion. Working on a sewing machine, she appliquéd enchantingly primitive cutout figures of angels and jaunty devils, all in brilliant colors of leftover calicos and complete with her own marvelous symbolism. In her Last Supper scene, all the apostles are dressed in white except Judas, whose drab clothing no doubt was designed to suggest his character.

Mrs. Powers exhibited one quilt at the 1886 Georgia Cotton Fair in Athens, where it caught the eye of Miss Jennie Smith, one of the townspeople. At the time, Mrs. Powers refused to part with the quilt at any price, but four years later when she and her husband were in need of money, Mrs. Powers sought out Miss Smith and sold her the quilt for five dollars.

Masterpieces such as these were a rarity in young America. They were the work of a few artists who could envision an intricate design from a batch of leftover fabric. Most women favored the geometric designs of pieced work, which simply required a good eye for color and an ability to sew a straight seam. Those who preferred appliqué generally worked repeat designs, as illustrated by two of the winning quilts in the Great Quilt Contest, Autumn Leaf by Karen Hagen (page 68), and Butterflies by Mrs. Hugh Vaughn (page 69), in which each butterfly was pieced together and then appliquéd to the quilt top.

Particularly noticeable among quilts with a repeat design is the place superstition once held in quilt making. Quilters purposely included at least one irregularity in their handiwork to avoid offending God with any attempts

9

at perfection. Many an otherwise perfect quilt would appear with one out-of-place block. Early American quilts also often included such marks as the pineapple, a symbol for hospitality; the tulip, an omen of good luck, and the hex of the Pennsylvania Dutch.

Other quilts representative of early America were whole-cloth quilts in which the decoration was formed entirely by the quilting stitches themselves. Once our foremothers began spinning their own fabric, they made their quilts of linsey-woolsey, a fabric consisting of a linen warp and a wool weft. The name is derived from the Middle English *linsy wolsys*, which comes from Lindsay, a village in Suffolk,

Right: Appliquéd Garden of Eden quilt made by Abbey Bell Ross in 1874, New Jersey. Details above and below. Ben Mildwoff collection.

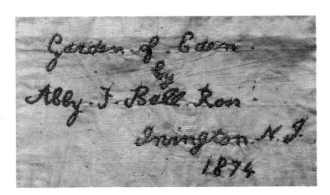

England, where the fabric was first made.

Many of the ladies aboard the first ships sailing for the New World wore linsey-woolsey petticoats, which were popular in Europe at that time. No doubt the colonists chose to weave this fabric because of its strength and warmth, rubbing it with a stone to give it a polished sheen. While these early linsey-woolsey quilts are called "whole cloth," more often they were made of strips or blocks of fabric joined together simply because their makers either did not have enough cloth or did not have home looms wide enough to weave an entire quilt top.

In dyeing their homemade fabrics, the ladies of the time had to rely on colors from nature: yellows from peach and pear trees, subdued browns from roots and tree barks. One of the most popular shades was indigo, from the leaves of the indigo plant, because it "took" well with linsey-woolsey. After the colonial housewife discovered that her indigo turned out darker and clearer when she used a dye pot made of iron, she often added nails and iron filings from the blacksmith's shop to her kettle to make sure she would end up with a true blue.

Later textile makers found they could produce a smooth, lustrous finish on linsey-woolsey with a glazing process of running the fabric under a hot press, a technique used on the quilt shown here, made in 1800. The strong colors of this quilt and the eight-pointed star (a favorite motif of quilters) are suggestive of the magnificent Amish quilts produced in the nineteenth century. An example of a typical Amish quilt appears on page 16. The Amish were forbidden by their religion to embellish their houses or themselves with anything purely decorative. They were permitted, however, to sew a quilt in glowing colors since their bedding was made in the name of thrift and practicality; surely the devil could not lead an industrious stitcher astray! The Amish quilts, often pieced "whole-cloth" quilts, were made with a central design—a star or a square—and fine, understated quilting that often complemented the design so that a star, such as the one shown here, might appear to be expanding beyond the limits of the actual piecing.

Ironically, the Amish quilts displayed some of the boldest and most dazzling abstract designs and the most original color combinations—brilliant reds and violets, turquoises and chartreuse greens—colors made even more pronounced by the Amish use of wool, which absorbed the dye and gave the colors a warm glow. Perhaps these color combinations could only be achieved by a group of people who were deprived of bright color in every other part of their daily lives.

Even the most pious settlers of the Old West, who scrupulously avoided bright colors, appear to have thought quilts were an exception. In the late 1800s, the daughter of a Baptist preacher was planning a quilt with her mother when she discovered that their scrap bag was low. They decided to go down to the dry-goods store to pick up a few pieces of bright calico.

"We had picked three pieces of remnant blue and was just fingerin' some red calico. We was jest plannin' on enough for the middle square from that.

"Just then Papa come in behind us and I guess he saw us lookin'. He just walked right past us like he wasn't with us, right up to the clerk and said, 'How much cloth is on that bolt?'

"The clerk said, 'Twenty yards.'

"Papa never looked around. He just said, 'I'll

Opposite: Variable Star, glazed linsey-woolsey, circa 1800, New England. 101" x 99" pieced quilt. The eight-pointed star in the center was a favorite motif of the time and has since become a classic. Museum of American Folk Art.

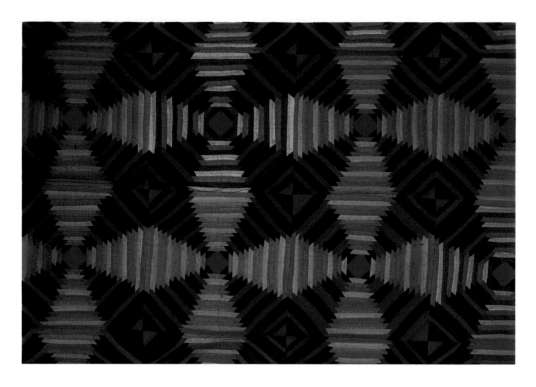

take it all!'

"He picked up that whole bolt of red calico and carried it to the wagon. Mama and me just laughed to beat the band. Twenty yards of red. Can you imagine?

"A Baptist preacher, jest like any other man, likes that red. We had red for a long long time."

In the middle 1800s, cloth was available in the East, but still scarce to the pioneer woman moving out West, and so the pieced quilt was the most frugal way to make mattresses and comforters for the family. The early days of the development of the West produced an explosion of pieced quilts of brilliant colors and very modern Op art effects, as in the Windmill Blade pattern shown here (also called Pineapple), in which the blades of the windmill actually appear to revolve. The seemingly insurmountable difficulties of building houses, rearing children, growing food, and making clothing in a wild, inhospitable country appear to have only encouraged the spark of creativity. The exuberant colors and geometric designs reflected the vitality of the times in a young country building and expanding itself.

Women who worked side by side with their husbands, building houses and plowing fields, constructed their quilts in the same way.

"There wasn't no choice about finishing this house. Mr. Thompson and I, we worked side by side all them years. Up till I was sixty-five, he taught me everything I know about building and carpentry. We was more than married; we was partners. When he died, we was in the middle of building this house for ourselves, and after the funeral I come home and put on my overalls and finished this house in thirty days. I never looked up till I was through. I lost fifty-seven pounds during that time. Then I took up quilting.

"I plan my quilts just like I used to plan a house. Folks say, 'How come you quilt so good?' I say, 'If you make careful plans, it will come out right.' "

Women isolated in the West traded designs with other women in their settlements and with travelling salesmen. They experimented with traditional designs and took their inspiration from shapes and colors around them: log cabins, straight furrows of plowed fields, and land as far as the eye could see.

"One time I made a Dresden Plate that like to never circled. I had them center edges about a

Above and opposite: Detail of 1850 Windmill quilt. Ben Mildwoff collection.

14

sixteenth of an inch off. I watched my Papa build a wooden windmill when I was little and he had the same problem. Oh, how beautiful that windmill was when he got it finished, standing up against the sky. It meant water, you know. But it really just looked pretty by itself . . . tall and with the top turning this way and that, whirring around.

"Back then I slept in the attic room. There was windows at each end and I had my bed under one of them. I could hear the windmill at night. That sound was my lullaby. The windmill seemed like the biggest circle then, bigger than the moon or a wagon wheel, and always in motion."

Even the names of quilt designs conjure up romantic images of the Old West: Drunkard's Path, Courthouse Steps, Log Cabin, Barnraising, Goose Tracks. They include games (Old Maid's Puzzle), square dances (Eight Hands Around), trades (The Dusty Miller), and most of all, the making of the West itself.

"Rocky Road to Kansas. . . . I guess they named it that for a purpose. People thought a lot about roads in the old days. Specially when they didn't have any. Seems the road got important enough to name a quilt after anyways. When you was in a wagon train and didn't have no road to follow. . .now that rocky road meant hard times to Kansas. But in them days when you made a road, the thing you remembered most about it was the rocks you had to move. Rocky Road to Oklahoma they sometimes call it too. Makin' new roads through the rocks.

"That country road out yonder is jest like a

Opposite: Bow Tie, Amish, circa 1910, Ohio. 88" x 72" pieced quilt. America Hurrah Antiques.

Above: Abstract crazy quilt, wool and flannel, 1900-1910, Lancaster, Pennsylvania, area. 78" x 73". Made by a country woman, this quilt shows an intuitive sense of the power of abstract design and color that is very modern. Museum of American Folk Art (private collection).

lifeline to me. A body just don't have to work near so hard, nor worry near so much when you know that the road is hard and dry. If you need to get to town, or if the doctor needs to get out here, it can jest be done."

The simple geometry of the pieced quilt was often made by dividing the whole area of the quilt into large squares or "blocks." Each block was then subdivided into smaller squares that could be used as the framework for an unlimited variety of geometric patterns—colorful kaleidoscopes of squares, diamonds, or hexagons. Quilters even made use of scraps and strings left over from other patchwork and joined them into large enough pieces from which to cut new shapes. Components of these "pieced piece" quilts could be as small as three-quarters of an inch square, and some quilts have been found to contain as many as 40,000 pieces.

All odd-shaped pieces of fabric that were too small for other uses were hoarded in scrap bags and ended up in quilts, or were traded with neighbors. Some were even handed down to future generations.

"I like to keep my pieces up. Don't do to have lots of little worthless pieces lying around. So when I get to the bottom of the bag, I make a string quilt. . . . You just pick up all the left-over pieces that's too small to cut a pattern from and you put them together however looks pleasing. . . . You can use up your strings

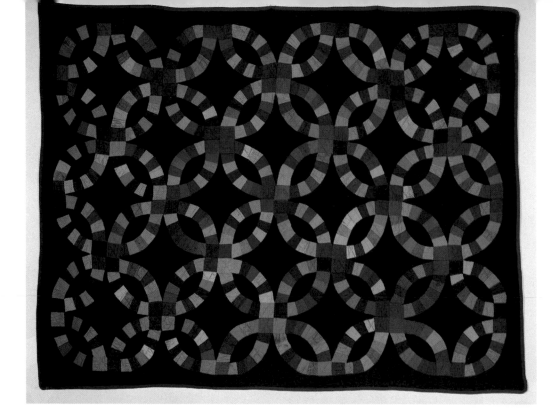

when you're just piecing for cover.

"Now these are for my sunlight and shadow in the Log Cabin. I'm gettin' close to the bottom on my lights. I've got plenty of darks. I have to keep my eyes open for lights. I always know what shade will match what I got in mind. I never buy for my piece bag, and I hate to borrow. I like to think I can take care of myself."

Both scraps and stitching expertise were passed on from mother to daughter (and often to son) as soon as the child could thread a needle and sew a straight line for piecing quilt tops. Young girls began at an early age to work quilt tops for their hope chests, no doubt fearful of the old adage embroidered on one quilt:

At your quilting, maids don't dally,

Quilt quick if you would marry,

A maid who is quiltless at twenty-one,

Never shall greet her bridal sun!

Each quilt top was numbered, reserving the thirteenth for the bridal quilt. But while the well-prepared country girl had her pieced quilt tops at hand, they were not quilted until her engagement party, when neighbors and friends would gather together to stitch the expensive backings. The design for the bridal quilt was planned by the bride (with a few tips here and there from the groom), but stitched by family and friends. Treasured patterns were the difficult Double Wedding Ring, shown

above, and the exquisite white on white trapunto quilt, similar to the crib quilt shown at right. All-white quilts were often decorated with hearts, which were not to be taken lightly back then and were reserved only for bridal quilts. The common superstition was that hearts used freely on quilts were sure to bring about a broken romance. Superstition also held that a broken vine pattern on a bridal quilt meant that the bride's life was sure to be cut short by disaster.

"When a girl was thinkin' on marryin', and we all done a lot of that, she had to start thinkin' on gettin' her quilts pieced. The way I done mine was real nice, I think. Papa had laid up a beautiful arbor with the brush he had cleared from the land. It was set up aways back of the house. Well, I jest went out under that arbor, set up my frame, and went to quiltin' outdoors. . . .

"Anyways, what I was doin' was settin' there under that quiltin' arbor one spring afternoon, April fourteenth, just quiltin' and dreamin' a

Above: Double Wedding Ring, circa 1920, Atlantic, Pennsylvania. 85" x 66½" pieced quilt. The interesting stained-glass effect is created by the use of different shades of vibrant colors against a black background. Museum of American Folk Art.

Opposite: Baby quilt, white muslin, quilted and stuffed, circa 1825. 33" x 28" with a 6" fringe. America Hurrah Antiques.

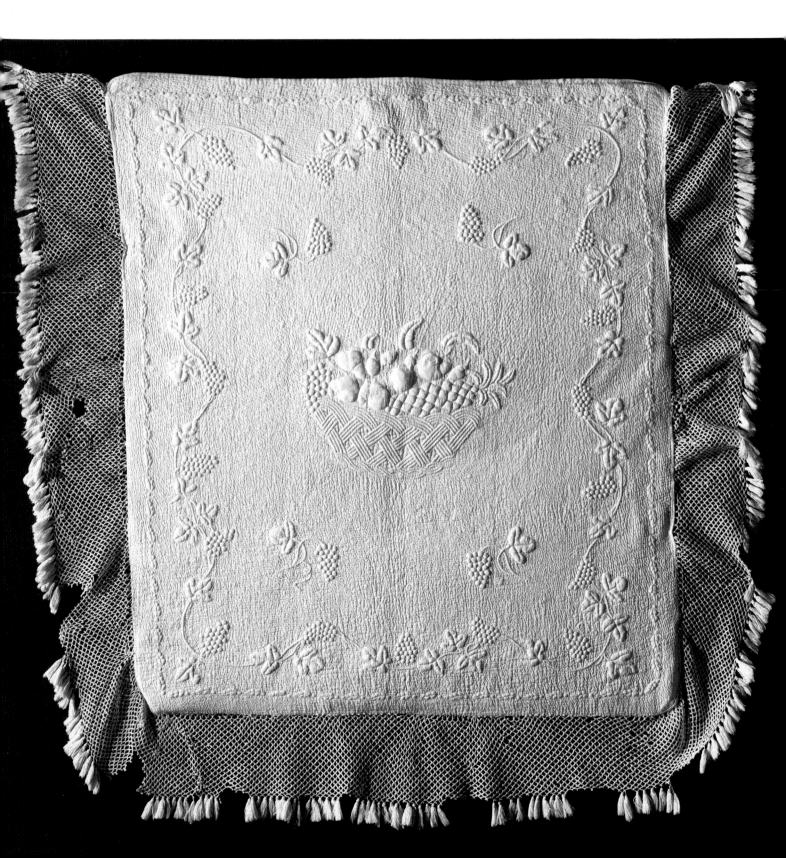

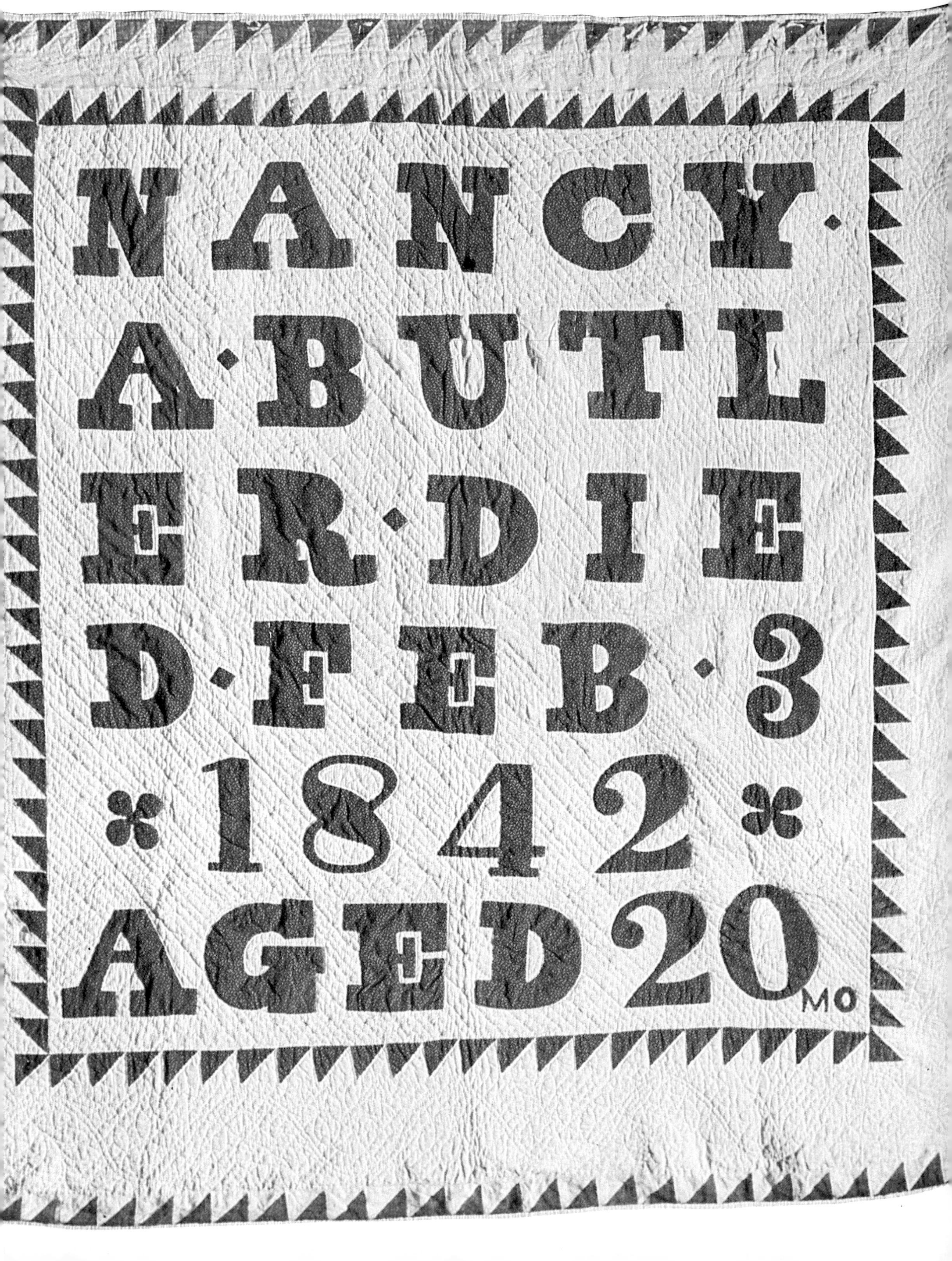
NANCY·
A·BUTL
ER·DIE
D·FEB·3
1842
AGED 20
MO

dream on ever stitch and just plannin' who might share 'em with me.

"And this deep, fine voice says, 'Pardon me, ma'am, but I've been seein' you out here every day for weeks and I jest got up my nerve to come over and speak to you and see what you were workin' on with such care.'

"Lordy, girl, I married him, and, as I recall it now, that was the longest speech he ever said at one time to this day."

Small wonder a bride was sent off to begin married life with a dowry of quilts, for quilts were indispensible in frontier life. They were used in place of doors and broken windows, as extra insulation around a four-poster bed, as bandages, mattresses, picnic blankets, and mats for infants at play, as payment during years when crops failed, or as a means of raising money at church bazaars.

" . . . Dr. Cooper was practicing medicine in Josephine then, and being the wife and nurse for a country doctor, I'd never had time nor need to quilt. We was often paid in quilts for services, and when I got more than we needed, I'd pass them out again. One time a big tornado struck the county and some of those little towns was leveled. Lord, it was a sad mess. I went along with Doc to nurse. I had stacks of quilts in the wagon ready right then for the emergency, and I was cutting them quilts up for bandages before the day was over. Some was used for bedrolls. Folks couldn't do any better than just to roll up and sleep right there on the ground so they could start rebuilding."

Quilts were often made to commemorate the death of a relative, as in the tombstone quilt

Opposite: Tombstone quilt made by Nancy Butler on the death of her granddaughter in 1842. Smithsonian Institution.

Right: Detail of an album quilt autographed in indelible brown ink given to a minister from his congregation. Smithsonian Institution.

shown here, made by Nancy Butler on the death of her grandchild in 1842. In another type, groups of quilters would sign in ink or stitch their signatures on an autograph quilt as a keepsake for a departing minister, teacher, or friend. A Methodist church in Ohio made a signature quilt, a detail of which is shown here, not only to present to their departing minister, but also as a means of raising money. They charged twenty-five cents a signature, and the finished quilt contained fifty-four squares filled with names.

During hard times—when a child died, or men were off to war, or a family was struggling to establish roots against unspeakable adversity—quilting was perhaps the only solace available to a woman, who was often comforted by the calm repetition of the stitching. In fact, in one woman's first year of homesteading in a sodhouse in barren Texas, planning quilts was the only reason she stayed at all.

"Mama said she thanked the Lord that the first dust storm didn't come up till late that

summer. *She would have turned right around and gone home if she'd seen one first off . . . Oh Lord. At the horizon the dust came up like a yellow band between earth and sky and then it kept on rising and rolling toward you till you were right inside it. . . . She hated being underground but she said at least you didn't hear the wind so loud. The sand would sift in through the door until you felt buried alive.*

"The first time Mama was left alone was when Papa hitched up the wagon to go after firewood. . . . The wind blew for three days so hard and the air was so full of dust that she had to tie a rope around her waist to get out to feed and milk the cow. There was nothing else but to endure it. She had never heard sounds like was in the wind. She took to quilting all day everyday. She used to say, 'If I hadn't had the piecing, I don't know what I would have done.' "

Quilting was also an excuse for women to socialize with neighbors who were often hours away by horseback. Quilting "bees" were as important a social event as a barn raising. They were not only a way to help out neighbors, but also a way to get the quilts stitched quickly. Groups of ladies would gather around the quilting frame, which was set up in the warmest part of the house, then happily stitch away while exchanging news, recipes, and quilt patterns.

Children were paid a penny a day to keep the needles threaded, and neighbors would sometimes refuse to go home until the work was done. Often entire quilts were finished in a single day. At the end of the bee, the unmar-

Below: Comic Characters, 1916, Middlefield, Massachusetts. 90" x 74" pieced and appliquéd quilt. This marvelous quilt was made on a farm during the winter of 1916 as a family project by the four children of Augustine and Jane Savery. The figures are based on comic-strip characters of the period. Thomas K. Woodward: American Antiques and Quilts.

Opposite: Schoolhouse quilt worked in cotton, circa 1900. Ben Mildwoff collection.

ried boys and girls would gather around the quilt and place a cat in the center. As each gripped an edge, they would fling the cat into the air, and the lucky person closest to the spot where the cat landed was next in line to become engaged.

Both quilting and quilting bees were by no means just women's work. Husbands and sons often helped with the quilt piecing, just as wives and daughters helped with the farmwork. Dwight Eisenhower and Calvin Coolidge are said to have helped their mothers piece together quilt tops, and there are several instances of couples quilting together. A husband in Texas was severely arthritic, but he could still hold a needle "right smart," and his stitches were indistinguishable from his wife's. Nevertheless, wanting to give credit where it was due, he insisted, "I only do the quilting. She's the artist. She's the one that makes the light shine."

Perhaps the reverse feeling was true with the white work quilt shown here that was made in the late 1800s. When Mrs. Joseph Granger won a bronze metal for it at a Massachusetts fair, Mr. Granger, disgusted with the time his wife had put into her quilt, set to work himself. A year later he came up with a similar quilt, proudly demonstrating how he'd saved so much time by using one of those newfangled sewing machines!

Modern invention notwithstanding, there is no replacement for those rare, handworked, all-white quilts. Such highly prized quilts were often done in the most breathtaking designs of stuffed work, or trapunto, which transformed a common piece of muslin into a masterpiece similar to the appliquéd and stuffed work quilt shown on page 25. Quilters sometimes even stitched narrow double lines of quilting and ran wool thread in between the lines, creating a raised "channel." In another approach to the same technique, quilters opened the coarseweave backing of the quilt with a stiletto and forced through tiny pieces of cotton to achieve a tightly padded effect. Designs such as those used for the Rose Wreath quilt—clusters of grapes, feather scrolls, vines, and overflowing baskets of flowers—were adapted from ones used in Europe, where trapunto had been popular for centuries. Quilters who were particularly skilled in white work made the tiniest of stitches, often requiring over a million stitches to cover the entire spread.

By the middle 1800s, album quilts were the rage among quilters, perhaps because settlers were doing so much moving around. They

Above: Crib quilt made by Mrs. Joseph Granger, circa 1878, Worchester, Massachusetts, with the bronze medal she won at a fair. Smithsonian Institution.

Opposite: Rose Wreath quilt made by Mary Palmer and her sister, Deborah, circa 1850, Otsego County, New York. 97" x 95", cotton, red and green on white. The appliqué is padded, and much of the quilting is stuffed. The center is a stuffed-work basket of fruit encircled by alternate wreaths of appliquéd roses and stuffed-work grapes. Smithsonian Institution.

were the autograph book of the nineteenth century, and, just like the autograph quilts, they were made to pay tribute to a bride, a friend, a minister, or even a young man reaching adulthood. Some of the most beautiful album quilts were worked in Baltimore, Maryland, as was the one shown here, but all were a communal project. Each block was worked and then dated and signed by the "donor." Album quilts often required two quilting bees, the first to plan the design, and the second to stitch and quilt the blocks together. But if the group were particularly daring, each lady would work on her own block privately, and then at the quilting bee, they would put the "surprise" package together.

"Two or three months after we homesteaded here in '90, Mrs. Wilcox told me about Pastor Williams. He was a big person in our lives—the traveling Methodist preacher. Well, a finer man you never saw . . . traveling those long distances from one part of the territory to another, and always helping out when he could. . . . He always just come and went . . . on to the next congregation that needed the word.

"Well, Mrs. Wilcox got the idea to put up a quilt for him. Something special. We only had time to quilt for cover in those days settlin' in . . . but in this quilt we did for the pastor we outdid ourselves appliquéing each one of us a block. And we sent out the word by him along the circuit for ladies of other congregations to send a design for the top; he could carry them little appliquéd pieces easy in saddlebags, no

weight to 'em. We gathered it all in and put that quilt together. That was a feat in those days. He said he never seen anything so pretty. It was a treasure."

A contemporary example of an album quilt was made to present to an entire town. Three generations of women in Goffstown, New Hampshire, created a quilt to commemorate the Bicentennial (page 84). Each woman worked a block depicting a different landmark of the town. One square is a scene of a team of oxen hauling large logs down a road, illustrating an edict passed by Queen Anne in 1710 that proclaimed Goffstown's white pines the most suitable to mast the Royal Navy.

Some enterprising album quilters worked all the blocks themselves and then had the blocks autographed by friends or the famous. In the last part of the nineteenth century, Mrs. Robert Yost worked nine years requesting scraps of ties from famous men and swatches of dresses from famous women. She managed to collect patches and uniform ribbons from such notables as President Ulysses S. Grant, Oliver Wendell Holmes, and Robert Louis Stevenson, who sent her a piece of fabric from Samoa, along with the following explanation:

Above and opposite: Album quilt, circa 1850, probably Baltimore, Maryland. 91" x 92" appliquéd quilt in cotton and velvet. There is a great deal of speculation about how and where these album quilts originated. Whether the separate motifs were drawn by a few people and purchased by many, or whether an entire quilt was purchased with the motifs already drawn in, is unknown. So many similar quilts have turned up in the Baltimore area, that it is assumed that the designs originated there. Smithsonian Institution.

26

"Dear Madam:

"I do not know that I have often been more embarrased [sic] than by the receipt of your amiable request. I have at the present moment two neckties in common, which I am vain enough to consider becoming. Earnest consultation with the ladies of my family leads me to believe that the colours of these neckties would not be found suitable for your enterprise. Besides which to part with any fragment of the two in question would inflict upon me a loss difficult to be retrieved. In these distressing circumstances it has been suggested that a portion of my sash might (if I might be allowed to express myself so trivially) fill the bill. I enclose accordingly a portion of this valuable fabric and I have the pain to inform you that in the act of separating it the sash (my only one) has been seemingly irrepairably damaged."

During the last quarter of the nineteenth century, patchwork was the rage in every household, but less for necessity than as a way for women to while away their increasing leisure hours. Packages of silk and satin remnants could be store-bought, commercial quilt-making kits were available, and magazines advised the proper ladies of the day that common fabrics such as calico were taboo.

True to tradition, the Victorian quilt maker saved scraps of clothing for her quilt, but since the fashions of the day were exotic velvets, silks, and brocades, Victorian patchwork was a collage of rich fabrics and splashy colors. Ladies worked fine feather and buttonhole stitching over these swatches—the more diverse the stitches, the better—then added buttons, bangles, beads, and Kate Greenaway figures, turning out quilts for everything from lap throws to piano stools. As more stitches

Opposite and above: Album quilt made by Pocahontas Virginia Gay, 1900. Smithsonian Institution.

and fabulous materials were added, quilt making became a game of one-upmanship among the women, and some of the most beautiful and fanciful examples of American embroidery were done during this period.

Even album quilts took a Victorian turn, as in the quilt shown here, a fabulous "portrait" album of the maker's "favorite things." It was worked in 1900 by Miss Pocahontas Virginia Gay of Virginia, a seventh-generation descendant of *the* Pocahontas and John Rolfe. It is a typically Victorian mix of appliqué, embroidery, and pieced work with some stenciled detail. She included finely embroidered animals, shown in the above detail, along with likenesses of Andrew Jackson, Jefferson Davis, Robert E. Lee, and, of course, her famous Indian ancestor.

Seventy-six years later, Mrs. Rhoda Fisher of Carson City, Nevada, traded in the Victorian silks and satins for a more contemporary material—blue denim (page 67). On pieced blocks of fabric cut from old blue jeans, she embroidered her daughter's favorite things.

An entirely different effect was achieved by Caroline Riddle of Gatlinburg, Tennessee, who worked a modernistic montage of her favorite crafts in appliqué and embroidery, complete with samples of weaving, a cornhusk doll, and even pieces of dyed yarn hung on a tree limb to dry (page 80).

Before the Victorian era, quilters discovered that, regardless of the fabrics used, there was more to patchwork than simple piecework; they found they could fold their patches for

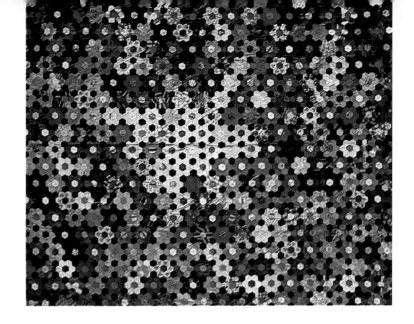

marvelous three-dimensional effects. They worked "yo-yos" or "bon-bons" by gathering circles of cloth, flattening them out, and then stitching them together for a rainbow of bright rosettes.

Among the most intriguing of all patchwork designs is Cathedral Window. (At least three from each state were entered in the Great Quilt Contest). The patches are folded to give a three-dimensional look, and the finished effect is a series of brilliantly colored stained-glass "windows" framed by the folded background material. They are made with printed fabrics for the folded squares and a solid material for the "windows" or vice versa (see page 136).

Another Cathedral Window pattern that is quicker and simpler to make than the original was often used in Victorian days. It is made by stitching together the four corners of Cathedral Window diamonds, which are bound and edged with contrasting fabric, leaving an openwork effect. A second color used as backing shows between each window. Regardless of the technique used to create the pattern, Cathedral Window is an intriguing design because the longer you look at it, the more the diamonds appear instead to be a series of interlocking circles, as shown opposite.

Opposite, top: Silk openwork Cathedral Window, circa 1900. Ben Mildwoff collection.

Opposite, bottom: Silk Yo-Yos, circa 1900. Ben Mildwoff collection.

Above: Flower Garden made of silk hexagons, circa 1850. Ben Mildwoff collection.

A more traditional pattern, but one that is just as interesting to create, is the favorite Grandma's Flower Garden, a seemingly random batch of flowers, each blossom composed of seven interlocking hexagons of similar colors.

"The way my first quilt come about had to do with growing. Before we was old enough to sew, Mama taught us to garden. She had nine kids and the field hands to feed, so she put in a big truck garden every year. All us kids had to work in that garden beginning around age eight; but before then, when we were just small, we each had a little flower garden to tend. Mama loved flowers, but she didn't have time to work them herself, so she put us little kids to learning gardening on flowers.

"Well, we quilted in the winter mostly. And when it came time for me to piece my first quilt, it was a Flower Garden. My fingers just wanted to work flowers. All the pieces in my first quilt was flowered prints."

The quilt above was made in the 1850s, but in 1976, Wanda Dawson gave grandma's idea a new twist by working hexagons into a "real" flower basket (page 51).

Whether flowered prints or surplus silk, Victorian quilt makers retained the ancient Chinese custom of stitching materials and mementoes of friends and relatives into their quilts, creating a vast canvas with a bit of history in every work. In 1889, a young girl named Lucy Larcom wrote of all the memories those patches conjured up for her:

"I liked assorting those little figured bits of

cotton cloth, for they were scraps of gowns I had seen worn, and they reminded me of the persons who wore them. One fragment, in particular, was like a picture to me. It was a delicate pink and brown sea-moss pattern, on a white ground, a piece of a dress belonging to my married sister, who was to me bride and angel in one. . . . I could dream over my patchwork, but I could not bring it into conventional shape. My sisters, whose fingers had been educated, called my sewing 'gobblings.' I grew disgusted with myself, and gave away all my pieces except the pretty sea-moss pattern, which I was not willing to see patched up with common calico. It was evident that I should never conquer fate with my needle."

The making of a quilt often spanned a lifetime. In fact, one turn-of-the-century quilter actually stitched in a likeness of herself when she started, then another likeness when she

finished the quilt thirty-two years later. When finally completed, the quilt was an autobiography—each section a memoir of the events that occurred while it was being made. Marguerite Ickis, a quilting enthusiast, remembers what her great-grandmother had to say about one such quilt:

"It took me more than twenty years, nearly twenty-five, I reckon, in the evening after supper when the children were all put to bed. My whole life is in that quilt. It scares me sometimes when I look at it. All my joys and all my sorrows are stitched into those little pieces. When I was proud of the boys and when I was down-right provoked and angry with them. When the girls annoyed me or when they gave me a warm feeling around my heart. And John too. He was stitched into that quilt and all the thirty years we were married. Sometimes I loved him and sometimes I sat there hating him as I pieced the patches together. So they are all in that quilt, my hopes and fears, my joys and sorrows, my loves and hates. I tremble sometimes when I remember what that quilt knows about me."

In the nineteenth century, Mrs. Decatur came up with a remarkable way to stitch her life into her quilt. She worked the traditional Log Cabin design with swatches from her fabulous wedding gown and ballgowns. At about the same time, a New York tailor made a similar quilt with remnants of lining fabrics from men's suits he had made.

Above: Log Cabin, Courthouse Steps design made by Samuel Steinberger, 1890-1900, New York City. 68" x 56" pieced quilt. Steinberger was a tailor, and his quilt is constructed from the remnants of satin and velvet fabrics used to line vests and coats. Museum of American Folk Art (private collection).

Opposite: Ball Gown quilt, Courthouse Steps design, made by Mrs. Decatur, circa 1900. The quilt is made of remnants of silks, satins, and velvets from Mrs. Decatur's ball gowns. Private collection.

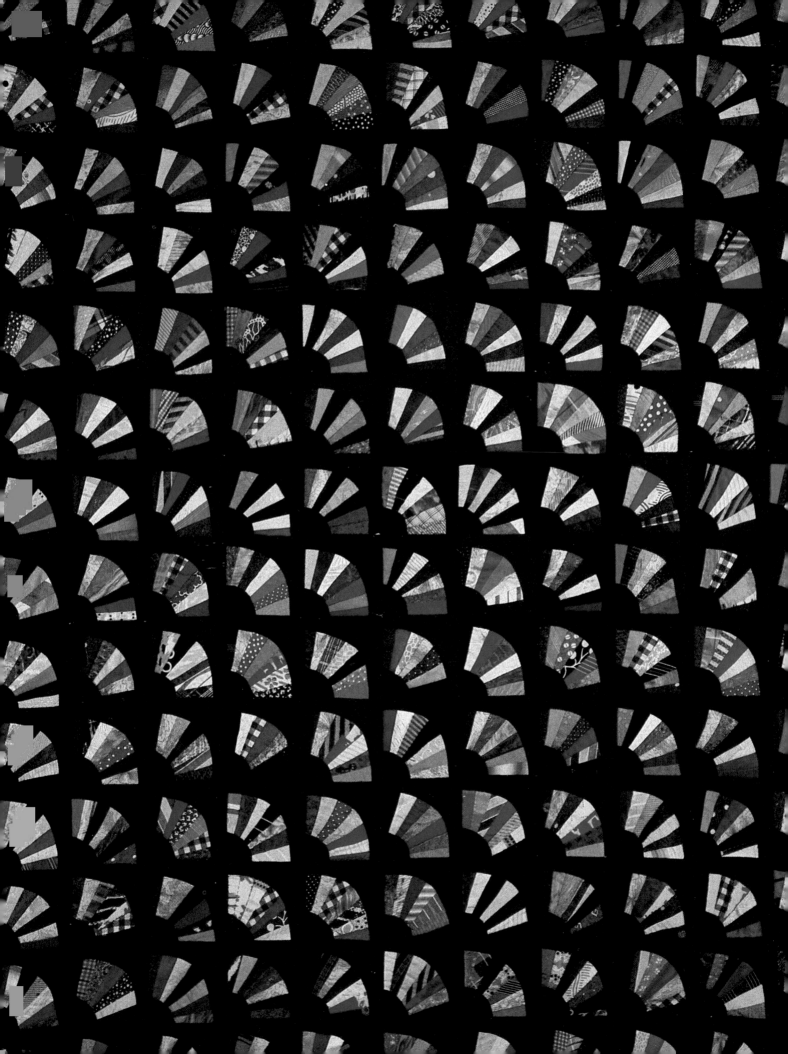

Quilts were even made as eulogies to life-times that had ended. Memory quilts were made a century ago from the pieces of clothing of a deceased family member or a friend with the name and date of death stitched in, along with a comforting phrase or verse. But by far the most ghoulish of such quilts was the Kentucky Coffin quilt, stitched by Elizabeth Roseberry Mitchell in 1839. Worked in subdued shades of tans and browns, the center of the quilt depicts a fenced-in cemetery containing caskets. The rest of the quilt is pieced and arranged in eight-pointed stars, presumably with fabrics from the clothing of departed relatives. On the border were appliquéd more coffins bearing the names of living family members. As each relative passed on, his casket was moved to the inner square!

Aside from the memory quilts, Victorian quilt patterns were anything but somber, and the ladies of the times delighted in embellishing the traditional patterns with a few unexpected twists. One of the most difficult but popular of

Opposite: Victorian Fan quilt pieced with black silk. Ben Mildwoff collection.

Above: Velvet and silk Courthouse Steps quilt with embroidery stitches. Ben Mildwoff collection.

all designs in those days was the Fan, and, along with a crazy quilt, every Victorian household had at least one fan quilt. Fan patterns were used to cover everything from borders to the centers of crazy quilts (as in the quilt on page 7), which were then finely embroidered with lilies of the valley, violets, and feather stitching to resemble oriental fans. For an even newer twist, see prizewinner Helen Lang's Fan (page 50), which is a striking combination of Fan and Double Wedding Ring patterns.

Other examples of Victorian embellishments on a traditional pattern were Log Cabin designs that were built around hexagons, rather than around squares. The result is an interesting optical effect that makes it appear as if the central shape is ever expanding.

Victorian quilters also added printing, stenciling, and painting techniques to their quilt tops. An outstanding example of these different methods is the centennial quilt on page 36. Along with album quilts, imaginative Victorian quilt makers used piecework as a literal autograph book, employing signatures or clever sayings or verses to make up the design itself, similar to the tombstone and signature quilts on pages 20-21, and the modern Q-U-I-L-T Spells Quilt on page 59.

35

It is no wonder that quilts, although used to commemorate everything from birth to death, were often a gesture of patriotic pride. While ladies did not yet have the right to vote, they could cleverly let their opinions be known by giving their quilts names like Clay's Choice and Lincoln's Platform, or by stitching out campaign slogans, or by making quilt tops out of political party handkerchiefs.

The tradition of creating a quilt as an expression of a political view is being carried on today in the Great Quilt Contest. A striking example is Marie Newdiger's Emancipation quilt (page 78), designed by Edward Larson. Other "political" quilts by the same designer include such popular subjects as Franklin Roosevelt, George Washington, Jesse James, and even one quilt commemorating Richard Nixon's resignation.

Quilts recorded battles and bombs bursting in air; they were decorated with liberty bells, eagles, flags, the Declaration of Independence, and with portraits of American heroes. On one quilt, a poem, elaborately inscribed in ink, mourned the defeat of the Whig Party after Henry Clay's loss in 1852:

As long as thy waves shall gleam in the Sun,
And long as thy Heroes remember their
Scars.
Be the hands of Thy Children united as one,
And peace shed Her Light on the Banner of
Stars.
Hail! Thou Republic of Washington, Hail!
Never may Star of thy Union wax pale,
Hope of the World! May each Omen of ill
Fade in the light of thy Destiny still.

Opposite and above: Pieced work, appliqué, and embroidery bedcover made for William W. Corcoran, founder of the Corcoran Gallery of Art, Washington, D.C., 1883. Fifty-six squares represent the states and territories of the United States, elaborately embroidered and painted. Smithsonian Institution.

Perhaps nothing provoked such a display of nationalism among quilters as the nation's one hundredth birthday. The quilt shown here is a masterpiece centennial quilt, worked in honor of William W. Corcoran, founder of the Corcoran Gallery of Art in Washington, D.C. It is made of fifty-six squares representing all the states and territories of the time, and each square includes the state flower with names and symbols elaborately embroidered in silk and fine gold thread.

One hundred years after the centennial, the bicentennial proved to be just as inspirational to many winners of the Great Quilt Contest. Teresa Barkley of Wilmington, Delaware, paired a bicentennial with a bridal quilt for her friend's marriage in 1976 (page 79). The Garden Club in Rockport, Maine, and the Avon Historical Society in Ohio worked album quilts similar to that of Goffstown's Heritage quilt (pages 84-85). Ruth Walker's America the Beautiful (page 87) provides highlights of America's history from the revolutionary war to the first Apollo moonshot.

Like the centennial quilts, each of the 10,000 entries in the Great Quilt Contest form a special patchwork of regional, national, and private histories.

"You can't always change things. Sometimes you don't have no control over the way things go. Hail ruins the crops or fire burns you out. And then you're just given so much to work with in a life and you have to do the best you

Fabric tapestries by Martha Mood. This page: Lotus, a portrait of Martha's dog; Rooster; and Chelsea Flower Girl. Opposite: Tenement. Reproduced with permission of her agent, Lester Henderson.

can with what you got. That's what piecing is. The materials is passed on to you or is all you can afford to buy . . . that's just what's give to you. Your fate. But the way you put them together is your business."

Today, as the evolution of quilt making as an art form seems to be gaining momentum, almost as many beautiful works in fabric are decorating our walls as are covering our beds. Of today's artists in this medium, few can compare with Martha Mood, whose exuberance and versatility were unrivalled. She had long been a collector of "found" objects, and her sculpture, painting, and still-life photography all demonstrated this talent for arranging elements in harmonious compositions.

Her particular medium was appliqué with

embroidery, using every imaginable kind of textured and plain material. Surprising patches would appear in her works—a piece of an army blanket, lace, ostrich feathers, buttons for animal's eyes, or a piece of someone's long johns. From the beginning, her creations reflected her remarkable feeling for balance, composition, and color.

The imagination and versatility represented by today's quilts are also evident in the quilts by Joan Schulze, one of the runners-up from California in the Great Quilt Contest.

Joan believes in staying flexible because as she works, her ideas about the final product change. In her design entitled California, she used batik (dying cloth by the lost wax method), then incorporated geometric piecing into a brilliant counterchange design.

Where Dreams Are Born literally represents its title. Joan had a very vivid dream one night and set to work at once translating it into fabric. Her subtle coloring is achieved by building layers of silk organza over one another and over other materials.

Karee Skarsten from New Jersey is typical of so many of today's artists whose imaginations seem unbounded. Her Niagara Falls is done with blueprinting on photo-sensitized cloth (technique on page 156). Wherever she lives, her quilts reflect not only her surroundings, but also her relations and reactions to them. Her prizewinning quilt Clouds (page 67) shows that power stations and pollution can be beautiful. In David's Rainbow, shown on page 42, a quilt made for her godson, a brilliant blue sky was painted and air brushed and the rainbow and clouds applied to produce a design in clear

Opposite: California, made by Joan Schulze.

Top right: Niagara Falls, made by Karee Skarsten.

Bottom right: Where Dreams Are Born, made by Joan Schulze.

primary colors—perfect for a child.

Bambi Mleczko's Nantucket, shown above, has a similar feeling. It combines traditional quilting techniques with vivid colors to produce a brilliant and direct contemporary design. In complete contrast is Madge Copeland's Under the Sea of Eden, a three-dimensional tapestry of colorful flowers and leaves. Seated on fish and with reins in their hands, riders representing members of her family are swimming through a glorious marine forest under a silver white moon. Madge believes that, "Although fine craftsmanship and technique play an important part, the *statement* is what makes the pieces art. My aim is to have my art reach out and convert the viewer into a participant."

Above: Nantucket, made by Bambi Mleczko.

Below: David's Rainbow, made by Karee Skarsten.

Right: Under the Sea of Eden, made by Madge Copeland.

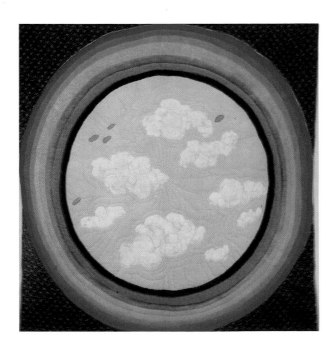

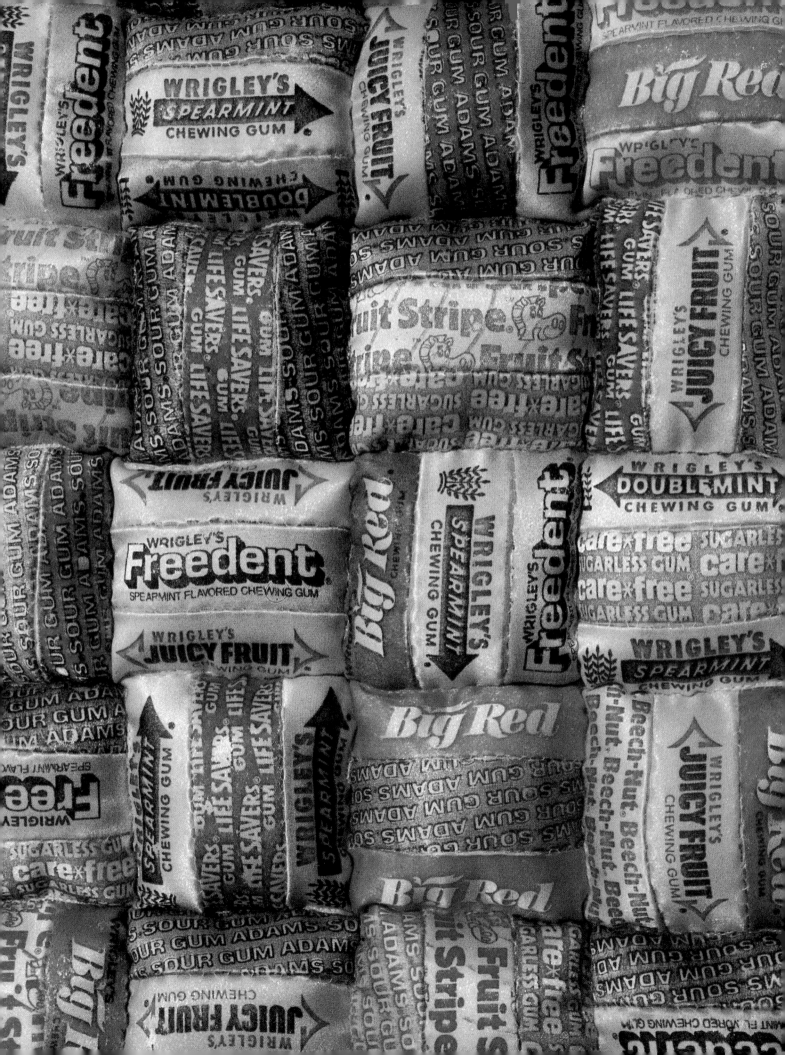

Susan Murphy from southern Illinois, creator of the Gum Wrapper quilt (page 44), was a runner-up in the Great Quilt Contest. She found that three gum wrappers joined together made a perfect square, from which she could create a Roman Stripe pattern, a traditional design of blocks laid vertically and horizontally, giving the effect of woven ribbons. For her unusual quilt, Susan photocopied gum wrappers, transferring the image to pastel colors of satin (technique on page 156), then pieced, padded, and quilted the squares. Susan has always been interested in the unusual effect of words and has made several other quilts, including one for a baby made with candy wrappers entitled Sweet Dreams.

Using traditional appliqué techniques but applying them to modern themes, Susan Wise, creator of the original and imaginative Inherited Differences shown above, became a runner-up from California in the Great Quilt Contest. Inherited Differences shows her mother behind a curtain, cake knife in hand, cutting the cake. Although each dessert slice is cut from the same cake, each is different, representing Susan and her brothers and sisters. Susan began teaching quilting when she lived in Appalachia. She says this hanging came about because she loves to work with ideas and, besides, she has a passion for chocolate! She has made several hangings in the same vein, all equally intriguing.

One of the most fascinating aspects of quilting is that, although America's fashions and lifestyles are continually changing, the tradition of quilt making has kept pace from generation to generation. America's development through each era has been paralleled by and is documented in her quilts. From colonial days to the era of the Revolution to the time the West was being conquered; from the Civil War to the centennial and then the bicentennial—all through these times, women have either proudly displayed their quilts as decorative possessions or used them only for warmth and hidden them under a store-bought spread. Fortunately, "loving hands at home" bears no stigma today. Homemade means the most valuable and precious of all things, and we are forever exploring new dimensions of design and pattern—all in the name of quilting.

Today's quilts are both museum works of art and treasured family heirlooms. They are hanging on walls as well as adorning beds and our clothing. And tomorrow's quilts are sure to reach an even more remarkable dimension as America's women continue to express their lives and dreams in fabric.

Opposite: Gum Wrappers, made by Susan Murphy.

Above: Inherited Differences, made by Susan Wise.

WINNERS OF THE GREAT QUILT CONTEST

Every quilt is a winner. The imagination and time and love that are the very fabric of a quilt make each creation an original—and a treasure. A contest is simply a means of sharing talents; the Great Quilt Contest enabled 10,000 quilters from all over the United States to share a piece of their lives with others interested in the art of quilting. Jinny Beyer was the national winner with her magnificent Ray of Light quilt. Through it she has gained the recognition she deserves as a gifted designer and teacher.

VIRGINIA
RAY OF LIGHT, Jinny Beyer

"The name of my quilt, Ray of Light, is the English translation of my daughter's Indian name, Kiran. I started with the central medallion, with rays of light coming from it, and began building my quilt around that. I think a quilt has to grow as it is made, graphing it out ahead of time seems to close the door to flexibility and improvement.

"My fabrics and colors were chosen simultaneously. My husband brought me several pieces of Indonesian batik a few years ago, and one was so beautiful that I wanted to use it in a quilt. I spread it out on the floor and went to my closet of fabric and pulled out every piece I thought would go with it. From there I selected specific ones that I wanted to use.

"I feel it is extremely important to remedy a mistake rather than continue, regretting what you have done. As a result, I am forever tearing things apart and putting them back together again or discarding completely and starting anew. One disaster I had was on a trip to California. I had quilted about three-fourths of my Ray of Light quilt and carried the quilt with me on the plane in a bag. At the last minute I . . . shoved my make-up bag into a side pocket of my carry-on bag. When I got to California I discovered that my hair spray had leaked and made a huge navy blue spot on my quilt and had faded all the fabric it touched. . . . I had to take a whole section of my quilt apart and piece new fabric into it.

"When I got a letter saying my quilt was one of the finalists in the Great Quilt Contest and that I must have the quilt in New York no later than October 31, I still had at least one-fourth of the quilting to do. I literally quilted twelve hours a day for those two weeks. I think my only salvation is that I am ambidextrous and can quilt with both hands!"

Pattern on page 160.

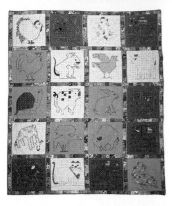

NEW YORK
DRAW ME, Linae Frei

"The idea of the design came from the numbered dot drawings in children's books. Each animal design is composed of straight lines connecting the pearl buttons (replacing dots), then embellished with appliqué and surrounded with bright patchwork. The idea of creating animals with just straight lines and the dot limitation held a lot of playful appeal to me, and after making a few samples, the idea developed into a large size quilt."
Pattern on page 166.

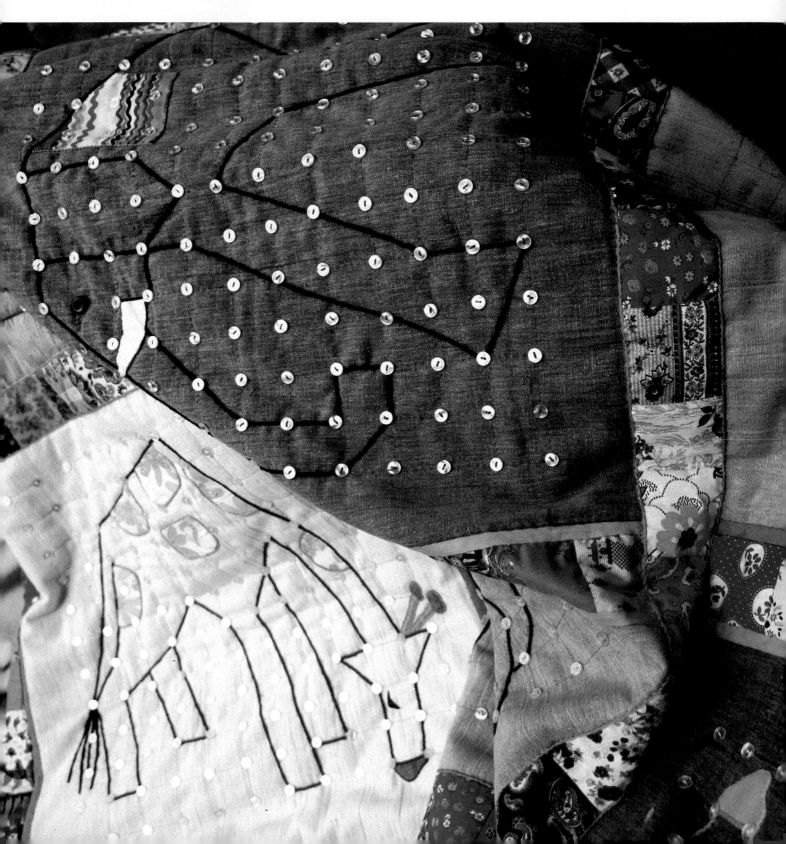

Top left: KENTUCKY
KENTUCKY LILY, Lucille Cox

Lucille bought a pillow with the Lily pattern on it from a "90-year young" lady, who had brought it from eastern Kentucky. Lucille chose lovely subtle colors and quilted it magnificently, using over 1200 yards of thread to work the design. She has been quilting for seventeen years.

Bottom Left: NORTH DAKOTA
FAN, Helen Lang

Helen's boldly colored quilt is an imaginative combination of two very traditional patterns: Fan and Double Wedding Ring. Her color choices and arrangement give her design an almost Op art effect, a look enhanced by her exquisite quilting.

Opposite: **NEBRASKA**
GRANDMA'S BASKET OF FLOWERS, Wanda Dawson

This bright quilt was made as a wedding present for Wanda's granddaughter, using many pieces of materials from clothes she had made for her as a child. Quilters discovered long ago that the hexagon shape made a perfect flower head, and called designs using the shape Grandma's Flower Garden (see page 31). Wanda's own version of the traditional pattern could be equally attractive made with squares or circles (Yo-Yos).
Pattern on page 170.

Far Left: **UTAH**
WINNER'S CIRCLE, Yukon Norman

Yukon painted the horse's head on the fabric, then pieced and appliquéd the rest by machine. The tan fabric background is tied with dark brown, giving it the effect of a horse blanket. Yukon says her husband and family are involved in racing horses, so the horse theme came quite naturally.
Pattern on page 172.

Left: **WYOMING**
NOAH'S ARK, Linda Hibbert

Living at the base of the Grand Tetons in western Wyoming, Linda finds that "animals are everywhere. There are deer in the backyard all the time, and as long as I can remember I have loved animals." Using simple outlines from children's coloring books, she painted the animals on the fabric and then quilted around the designs.

53

Opposite: **CONNECTICUT**
SCHOOLHOUSE CRAZY
QUILT, Mara Francis

Mara says she arrived at her design "like a jigsaw puzzle . . . putting a few houses together created a village, and then the roads and trees just blended in." Using her favorite "earthy" shades, she worked her quilt in wool, an ideal choice for its texture and warmth of color.
Pattern on page 178.

Right: **COLORADO**
CENTENNIAL COLORADO,
Joan Augustus Dix

Joan drew her inspiration "from the mountains—their grandeur and beauty." She worked in three sections, the ground, the middle, and the sky, drawing the shapes with tailor's chalk and appliquéing them by machine. "This quilt was the answer to the frustration of trying to paint the mountains in watercolor."

Left: NEW MEXICO
VICTORIAN CHILD'S QUILT,
Elaine Wiggins Howe

Elaine started with a small sketch of her quilt design, enlarged it to full size, cut out the pieces from brown paper, and then arranged and re-arranged the shapes to make a pleasing design. She chose her fabrics from a large collection of remnants, using textures and colors that were most suited to the design and feeling of a child's room.

Opposite: **GEORGIA**
TRAINS, Lois B. Moss

Lois chose trains for her design because as she says, ''My grandson is a train nut.'' Working from historical books, she simplified and enlarged the antique train shapes, then cut them out of lively colors and appliquéd them to the background. The oldest trains appear at the top of the quilt with the newer designs at the bottom, and the border is made with trains running along the tracks. Even her quilting designs worked between the rows of appliqué are in the shapes of trains.

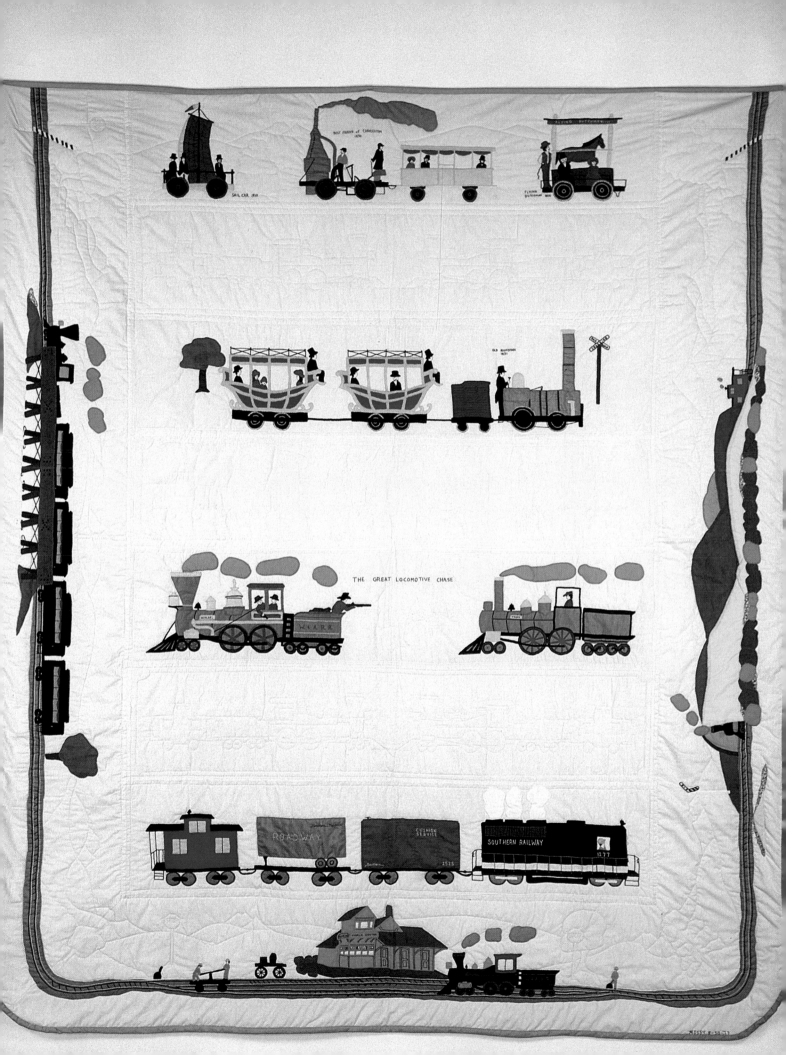

Opposite: **PENNSYLVANIA**
Q-U-I-L-T SPELLS QUILT, Nancy
Kountz

At first glance, this quilt appears to be a modern abstract design in melodic colors. Look more closely and you will discover that the word *quilt* is spelled out whether you read it from top to bottom or left to right! Nancy says she has been interested in letter forms as a design source for some time, and her graphic pattern beautifully illustrates just how the simplest shapes can be worked into a striking design.
Pattern on page 182.

Left: **MARYLAND**
LABELS, Pauline S. Hancock

"For some time I had been removing and keeping woven labels. The variety of shapes, the combination of colors, and the endless information on each label amazed me. Each seemed a bit of present or past history. They came from many countries, states, and cities; many manufacturers; department, mail order, and famous name stores. And they came from many articles: a mattress, shoes, boots, hats and caps, luggage, carpets, bedspreads, towels, and almost all garments from babies, children and teens to adults. Friends and relatives added to my store while I mulled over what exactly I'd do with them. A niece saw the Great Quilt Contest announcement and said, 'Aunt Polly, this is it. Get going.' "

DUTCH ELM AND LIVE PINES, Cynthia Veach
Espe

"I live in a town whose streets are lined with elms
so large that they arch across the streets and touch
each other. And, for me, one of the most awesome
and beautiful sights is the thousands of acres of
pine forests that carpet northern Minnesota. The
trees of both these areas were the inspiration for my
quilt."

Above: **SOUTH CAROLINA**
SUNRISE, Arvena L. Morgan

Arvena made her first quilt when she was twelve
years old. Growing up in the mountains of Tennessee, she wanted to do a quilt involving the mountains and the sun of the South.

Top right: **ALASKA**
MOON OVER THE MOUNTAINS, Rita D. Johnson

Living in Alaska "where the nights are beautiful
and where the moon gently frames the mountain
peaks" was a natural inspiration for Rita's interpretation of a traditional pattern. Rita has plans for
making every member of her family a beautiful quilt.

Bottom right: **FLORIDA**
BEACH SOLITUDE, Ann Humphries

Ann is a self-taught quilter, having grown up in
the Carolinas "where quilting is a way of life." When
she moved to Florida, she wanted to design a quilt
that said "sun, sand, and clear skies." After she
chose the design, she says, "the design chose the
colors."
Pattern on page 184.

RHODE ISLAND
SUNSET SEA, Margaret G. Boesch

Margaret based her idea on the traditional quilt design, Storm at Sea, adding stars and interpreting the design to express "the relationship of all things in life." It was made as a "frustration" quilt because she felt it would be a good idea to have something to work on during the inevitable frustration of building a house. This meant she worked on it in long and short spurts between building. Her description of "cool greys contrasted by warm rusts" does not do justice to her brilliant color choices and the interesting juxtaposition of the colors. They seem almost to glow against the background of the old post office at the Smithsonian Institution.
Pattern on page 188.

Left: IDAHO
SEMINOLE INDIAN QUILT,
Gayle J. Dixon

Gayle is twenty-eight years old and made this quilt when she was working as a Forest Service lookout during the summer. The design is a combination of traditional Seminole patchwork motifs and Navajo weaving patterns. Her brilliant colors are dramatized further by the sheen of polished cotton against the rich dark background.
Pattern on page 192.

Right: WASHINGTON
ELIZABETH'S FRIENDS,
Melinda Phillips

"Children's art is fascinating to me. It has a certain freshness that is hard for adults to recapture." For Elizabeth's Friends, Melinda used some of her daughter's drawings and worked with fabric dyes. To keep the childlike feeling, she let the designs cover the whole top, and quilted with large black stitches.

65

Opposite: **CALIFORNIA**
WIND AND WINDMILL, Marge Aguirre

"I love windmills. I also love the wind. After I appliquéd the windmill, I wanted to include the wind but wasn't sure how. Then my husband suggested quilting the faces of the wind and also the swirls, which I did, not knowing how it would look till I took the quilt off the frames."

The suggested profile of a face blowing swirls of wind is clearly visible in the lower left of the picture opposite. Marge even stitched the mill itself with khaki thread to suggest its rustic quality. ("You know, paint peeling off!")

Top right: **NEW JERSEY**
CLOUDS, Karee Skarsten

"Clouds illustrates my love-hate relationship with New Jersey, where the factories and even the smog can be beautiful," says Karee, for whom fabrics and new techniques are the tools of creative genius. She loves to experiment with techniques such as painting on cloth, blueprinting, screen printing, and batik. Another of her creations is shown on page 41.

Bottom right: **NEVADA**
NOSTALGIA, Rhoda Fisher

"Instead of Nostalgia, this quilt should be called re-cycling," Rhoda suggests, because she made the quilt for her daughter entirely from blue jeans. Each square is embroidered with an illustration of an experience in her daughter's life, such as a tooth because her daughter is a dental hygienist, and strawberries because the family once raised and sold them. All are stitched in cotton thread with a leather needle, which was easier to push through tough blue jean fabric.

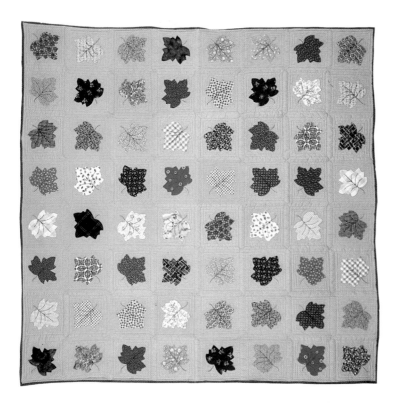

Left: **WEST VIRGINIA**
AUTUMN LEAVES, Karen Hagen

Karen placed her autumn leaves at different angles on her quilt so that they would have a "random, blown-about look." The contour quilting surrounding each leaf overlaps the framework of diamonds, making the leaves appear to float.
Pattern on page 194.

Opposite: **SOUTH DAKOTA**
BUTTERFLIES, Marjorie Vaughn and Laura Coleman

Marjorie first pieced her butterfly shapes, using both old and new fabrics, then appliquéd them to the background fabric, unifying the design with a soft green border. Laura quilted the design once the appliquéing was completed.
Pattern on page 196.

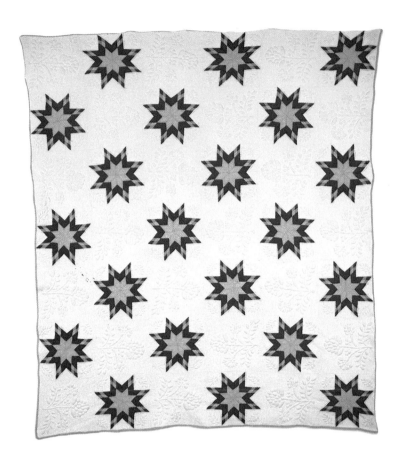

Left: **INDIANA**
RISING SUN, Helen Downs

Helen took a traditional sunburst pattern and created a masterpiece with her excellent piecing and quilting. She quilts on her own, and has never used a book. She uses a standing floor frame with rachets and #8 "blood" needles that she says are impossible to find anymore.

Top right: **MISSISSIPPI**
KENTUCKY'S TWINKLING STAR,
Vera King Russell

Vera made this quilt for her husband, reproducing the same exquisite design her great aunt had made before 1840. The piecing was done first, then the trapunto, and finally the quilting. Vera and her mother worked together during the many hours of stitching.

Bottom right: **ILLINOIS**
SUNRISE, SUNSET, Amy
Gehlbach

Amy quilts the way her mother did—with emphasis on perfection. "For as long as I can remember, my mother made quilts. I remember several days before my mother died and I was home for a few days. She had a quilt in the frame and some friends came to call and wanted to help her quilt. She didn't have the heart to tell them 'no,' but after they left, she took all the stitches out because they didn't suit her."

This quilt reflects Amy's love of nature. Once she had decided on the pattern and found the materials (which took the longest amount of time), it took her only one week to cut out all the pieces, two weeks to piece the blocks and set them together, and four weeks to quilt—a total of seven weeks to create her masterpiece.

71

Left: **MICHIGAN**
MY GARDEN QUILT, Walla
Doleski

Walla laid out her patterns on a double bed, constantly shifting the shapes around until she found the most pleasing design. Behind each flower, which is framed by a small diamond, she worked straight line quilting, but in the solid white diamonds between the flower rows, she quilted feather patterns. She remembers that she accumulated "considerable quantities of fabric" to get her lovely color effect, which is truly in keeping with the quilt's title.
Pattern on page 198.

Opposite: **ARIZONA**
TRAPUNTO II, Rheba J. Wright

"I wanted the design to be simple, elegant and classic, so I chose an off-white fabric and kept the whole pattern monochromatic. Working with double-knit fabric was a departure from the traditional, but it gave the whole thing a sculptural yet soft, squashy feel." The sculptural quality is enhanced by the trapunto padding used in certain areas.
Pattern on page 204.

Left: **WASHINGTON, D.C.**
LEDA, Janny Burghardt

Janny started with a single piece of fabric—a sheet with a design of waves—which inspired her beautiful and romantic illustration of the Greek myth, Leda and the Swan. Her restricted palette of blues and browns gives strength to the flowing forms and gives the entire design a feeling of Art Nouveau. The appliqué is done by hand. Janny says she likes to do as much piecing and quilting as possible by machine because she can see the design take shape quickly, like a painting.
Pattern on page 206.

Right: **NORTH CAROLINA**
FRENCH BOUQUET, Erma H. Kirkpatrick and Cuba Tracewell

The quilt top (a design from the Nancy Page column of the *Indianapolis Star,* 1933) was a gift to Erma from Cuba Tracewell, a neighbor, who was seventy-five years old and childless and wanted the top to go to someone who would appreciate it.

"The exquisite top inspired my best quilting. I quilted bouquets similar to the appliquéd ones and added butterflies and a background of small squares. The best part for me has been Cuba's delight that our quilt was selected the North Carolina winner in the Great Quilt Contest. She says that every morning she thanks God that she gave me the top. She wears the winner's medal around her neck and tells persons who inquire that she won it in the Boston Marathon. What's more, at age 79, she is now making blocks for another appliquéd quilt (Iowa Rose) for me! She measures the time it takes for each block by the number of soap operas she watches while she works."
Pattern on page 208.

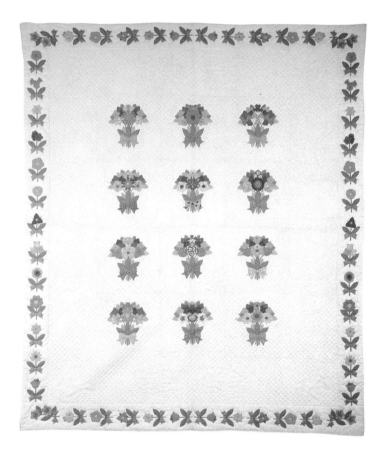

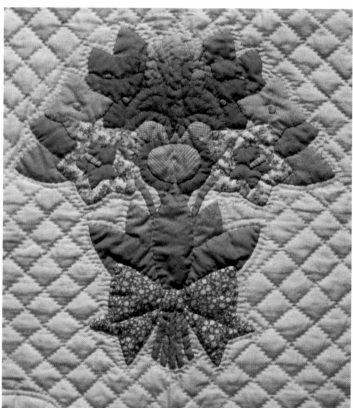

Left: MASSACHUSETTS
LISA'S QUILT, Lisa Courtney

A sensitive and gifted artist, Lisa seemed to have been born with a crayon in her hands. From simple "streams" of fabric she made this contemporary quilt, working with showers of melodic colors. Lisa originally entitled the quilt Confetti, but it was renamed by her family after Lisa's tragic death just before her twenty-fourth birthday. Her imaginative quilt is a fitting tribute to her creativity and talent as an artist.

Above: MONTANA
KEEPSAKE QUILT, Margorie H. Cannon and Josephine Moss

Starting with four blocks from a traditional album quilt, Marjorie then added her own personal keepsakes and symbols of important things in her life. The quilting was exquisitely done by Josephine. Marjorie took four years to do the top, adding each square as she came up with an idea for it. The Great Quilt Contest was her incentive to finish the quilt; she says she would otherwise have willed it to her daughter to finish.

Right: ALABAMA
CAMELLIA CAMEO, Annie Sellers Davis

Starting with the camellia, the state flower of Alabama, Annie says her quilt "just grew into a garden of flowers with a few birds and butterflies."

"I seldom plan the overall layout. Usually I start with an idea and the design develops as I work on it."

Above: **MISSOURI**
EMANCIPATION, Marie Newdiger

Marie has "been quilting since I was very young, helping my mother. She is eighty-six years old and still loves to quilt with me. For this quilt I used a nine-foot-long wooden frame which is over one hundred years old and belonged to my husband's grandmother."

Edward Larson designed Marie's Emancipation quilt. "I began this project because I wanted to see more and more people doing picture quilts. I have done more than two dozen in this way, and Mrs. Newdiger and I have finished six. My choice of a theme is usually a folk history figure. I have done quilts about Franklin Roosevelt, George Washington, Jesse James, and even a Nixon resignation quilt."

Opposite, top left: **TEXAS**
BRIGHT MORNING STAR, Vickie Milton

Vickie combined traditional patterns to make her design, experimenting first with colored pencils on graph paper, filling a forty-page book with sketches before arriving at the final design. She chose the colors for their Christian symbolic meaning: green for hope and victory, gold for joy and glory, red for love and suffering.

Opposite, top right: **DELAWARE**
BICENTENNIAL BRIDE'S QUILT,
Teresa Barkley

Teresa is twenty-two and has been quilting since she was twelve. When Teresa's friend Trisha was married in 1976, she realized the quilt she had begun as a gift would be a perfect bride's quilt. Every block has special significance to the bride, such as a square made from Trisha's dress and labels representing a newspaper with the wedding announcement as its headline.

Opposite, bottom left: **KANSAS**
PENNSYLVANIA DUTCH PARENTS'
QUILT, Chris Wolf Edmonds

Chris chose Pennsylvania Dutch symbolism to represent all the things she wanted to say about her parents, for whom she made this quilt: the oak leaf for strength and longevity, the bridal wreath for love, and the sprays of flowers for faithfulness. Nesting and flying birds illustrated Chris' inscription, "Presented to my parents, who have lovingly given their children two priceless gifts: one is roots, the other, wings."

Opposite, bottom right: **VERMONT**
STARS OVER AMERICA, Lucile B.
Leister

Lucile began her first major project with as many different star patterns as she could find that incorporated names of states and cities across the country: Texas Star, Indiana Puzzle, Union Star and Arkansas Traveller (also known as Cowboy Star).

"I guess I've been bitten by the bug. Quilting is a disease, you know, and I certainly hope no cure is ever found because the pleasure for thousands of quilters surely must be continued forever."

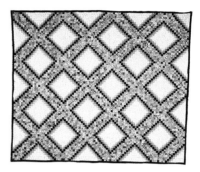

Opposite: **WISCONSIN**
CROSSHATCH, Anna Werner

The extremely fine piecing of tiny squares of pastel fabrics, the concentration of colors in wide diagonal design bands, and the fine quilting of each central diamond make this beautiful quilt a classic. Sadly, Anna Werner died at age 90 without knowing her quilt had won the award for Wisconsin, but her ingenuity will be a treasure for generations.

Top left: **TENNESSEE**
QUILTED MONTAGE, Caroline Riddle

This quilt represents the wonderfully productive craft region of Appalachia, and in particular the Pi Beta Phi Craft School in Gatlinburg where it was made. "Surrounded by a community rich in fine craftsmanship—furniture making, broom making, cornhusk work, weaving, basketry—it was only natural to represent this and to record it for others as a heritage to treasure and preserve."

Bottom left: **ARKANSAS**
CHERRY TREE, Berta Smith

Berta was married in 1919 when she was seventeen. "Soon afterwards I began quilting for necessity, and I have been continuously quilting since then—now I think it's for pleasure and pastime." She has seven children, twenty grandchildren, and eight great-grandchildren, and has made each of them a quilt.

OREGON
HATS AND PATCHES,
Susan Jane Franklin
Jones

Susan made this, her first quilt, in a class. She had been quilting for only a year and a half when she entered the contest, and has now collected the fabrics for a companion quilt with appliquéd blocks displaying men's hats.

82

Above: LOUISIANA
ENGAGEMENT RING, Margaret C. Brown

Margaret started quilting because she felt it was becoming a lost art. Although self-taught, she has helped and taught several hundred others to quilt. Her daughter chose the design, but since Engagement Ring was her first quilt, she says modestly, "My methods have improved with experience."

Right: **HAWAII**
PIKAKE AND TUBEROSE, Hannah Kuunililani Baker

The Hawaiian quilt, or *kapa,* is fashioned of two whole pieces of cloth, appliquéd in a free-style Island motif, usually in one color on white. The unique design on Hannah's quilt, made 40 years ago, is achieved by folding and cutting the fabric in much the same manner that a child would cut snowflake designs out of paper. The quilting, done freehand, follows the pattern, giving it a grace and rhythm characteristically Hawaiian.

Top left: **OHIO**
MEMORIES OF AVON, Avon Historical Society

Betty Sheak, who worked three of the blocks, drew all of the designs on cloth from photographs, and then thirty-eight Avon women cooperated to create the quilt. The quilt, on permanent exhibition in Avon's town hall, represents Avon's present, with blocks depicting farms run by descendants of the first settlers and the graveyard on the old Indian burial ground. It also represents Avon's history with scenes of things no longer existing: the pump, watering trough, weighing scale, and the first millinery shop and dry goods store.

Opposite: **MAINE**
BICENTENNIAL, Rockport Garden Club

Members of the club chose their designs and appliquéd, embroidered, and quilted their blocks by hand. The squares were then unified with bands of bright red and stitched together by machine for strength.

Bottom left: **NEW HAMPSHIRE**
HERITAGE QUILT, Goffstown Historical Society

Three generations of Goffstown women commemorated the bicentennial by presenting this beautiful album quilt to their town. Each woman worked a block depicting a particular landmark—often one in which they were somehow historically connected!

Left: IOWA
MY WAUKEE QUILT, LaVerne Jones

LaVerne designed, appliquéd, embroidered, pieced and quilted this memory of her town in four to five months. "I went around town and drew the designs. When some were complete and I compared them with the actual scene, I sometimes went back to try again!"

Occasionally skies were dyed to get the exact color. The Americana theme is suggested by stars and stripes in the quilting, and hearts quilted in the sky above LaVerne's own farm tell a story without words.

Opposite: OKLAHOMA
AMERICA THE BEAUTIFUL, Ruth Walker

Vance Walker, aged twelve in the bicentennial year, asked his grandmother to make him a quilt for his birthday. This quilt, with eighteen blocks tracing the history of America from the Mayflower to the space capsule, is the beautiful result. Ruth had the clever idea of "building" each of the designs from squares and triangles of color like a mosaic, working out the patterns on large scale graph paper (called quadrille paper).
Pattern on page 212.

IDEAS & METHODS

On the preceding pages you have been introduced to the working experience of many of the 51 prizewinning quilters. As each of them gives you her own approach to creativity, you can readily see that there is no single route to achieving a design.

One quilter likes to work with cutouts of colored paper, another with crayons and graph paper, while a third feels that the fabrics themselves are the best starting point for the design. For others, the design is controlled by a place or an event they want to commemorate; and many follow an existing pattern or an idea, adding their own personality in the combination of materials or in the way the quilt is set together or quilted. By examining the winning quilts and understanding the techniques used, you can choose the designs and methods that best suit your style and experience.

You will notice the one element that all the winning quilts have in common is that each is a strong individual statement. Because of the tremendous wealth of fabric textures and colors available today, no two quilts are ever alike, even though the pattern may be identical. New approaches and ideas are constantly appearing, for as Cynthia Veach Espe, winner from Minnesota, so aptly puts it: "Though quilting is such an old art, it is also new, with many frontiers left to explore."

In planning the "how to" part of this book, I decided to begin with the final part—the quilting. My reasons for this were reinforced when a letter arrived from Lucille Cox, the prizewinner from Kentucky, who has worked since 1966 with a group of quilters near her home in Lexington. She says:

"I think most quilt books and most teachers start at the 'wrong end' of the process. I think they should first learn how to put a quilt in the frame and quilt it. In this way they would learn that their seams must be uniform, the blocks

Donna, Beth, Edie, and Erica quilting in the New York studio. Quilt in brown velveteen and corduroy entitled Birds In Air, designed and made by Sandi Dobson.

88

Strawberry Baskets, designed by Erwin Rowland.

carefully matched, and the top must lie flat without wrinkles or puckers in order to be quilted. We get many tops to quilt which are put together crooked, puckered at seams, uneven blocks, etc. These errors are hard to correct, and if the top does not come out straight and flat, it will not look right after it is quilted. Most people do not realize these 'defects' when they sew the pieces and blocks together unless they know how it should look when stretched on the quilting frame."

Your design choice will naturally be influenced by the technique you plan to use, and if you are just beginning to quilt, you may find that there are a bewildering number of methods from which to choose. Therefore, it is best to start by making a series of small squares, or "blocks," as samplers. In this way, you can explore the various techniques and find your favorite approach to designing. You could then join the blocks together to form a sampler quilt. Not only will you have learned all the techniques of designing and constructing a quilt by making these squares, but you can also refer to the sampler quilt later to refresh your memory about techniques you may have forgotten.

Ruby McKim, writing in 1931, called quilting in blocks "apartment" quilting. In small rooms where it is difficult to set up a large quilting frame, the small squares are ideal. They can be pieced or appliquéd, stretched in a ring frame, quilted, and then joined. Ruby said her grandmother would have sniffed and said, "That's about as backwards as pickin' a chicken after it's baked." But

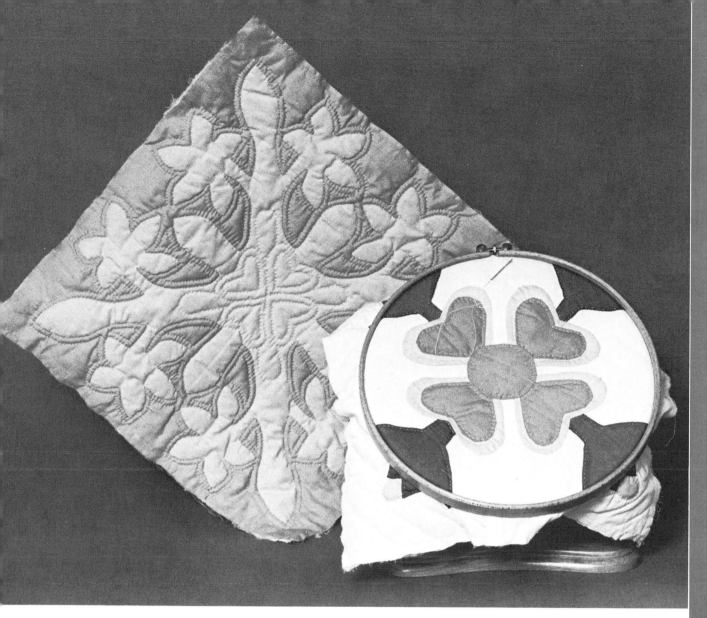

the small squares can easily fit under the arm of the sewing machine for machine quilting; they are portable and a great way, as noted before, for beginners to experiment without having to cope with yards of fabric. Our grandmothers first pieced or appliquéd their quilt blocks and then joined them to form a large single piece, which they then quilted on a square frame. The traditional technique is still preferred by many quilters because it allows more design freedom and keeps the whole quilt smooth and even. But in either method, it is the quilting stitches themselves that unify the design, covering and concealing the seams, whether the joins were made before or after the quilting of each block.

While our grandmothers' quilts were made primarily for warmth, the close, all-over stitching made the quilts practical, durable, and virtually crease-resistant—ideal for the easy lifestyle of today's America.

Sixteen patterns from the Great Quilt Contest have been included in this book. Because you will want to make the quilts in sizes to fit your individual desires and because amounts of fabric may vary according to their widths, no yardage requirements have been given. Suggestions about how to calculate your fabric needs, however, as well as directions for enlarging the patterns, appear on pages 130 and 159.

Your fabrics are your "paints," and they are much easier to select if they are filed in color ranges. Large pieces can be stored on cardboard bolts (available from fabric stores), small pieces in clear plastic boxes separating darks from lights, plain colors from prints. One hundred percent cottons, gingham, calico, and muslin "hold the fold" better than anything else and are easier to work with. Dacron and cotton blends are good for wash and wear; velvet and corduroy are good for tubular quilting and "whole-cloth" quilts. (Printed sheets in suitable designs are an excellent, inexpensive, quick way to make a "whole-cloth" quilt.) Always test materials by washing small pieces to check for color fastness and shrinkage.

When choosing prints, remember that the scale should balance the size of each patchwork piece. Plastic "templates" (patterns) are a great help here. You can move them about on top of the printed fabric and see exactly what the effect will be after cutting and piecing. (See *Tools* on the following page.)

Always buy more fabric than you think you will need to allow for mistakes and because you may change your mind and want more of a particular color as you go along. Once you are into patchwork, you will be making more than just one quilt, and you are sure to devise all sorts of ways of using up any extra pieces of fabric. Keep a "bit" bag that you can add to all the time. Pieces that have been cut to shape may be stored neatly by threading them together in a stack as shown, or by holding them in groups with a clothespin.

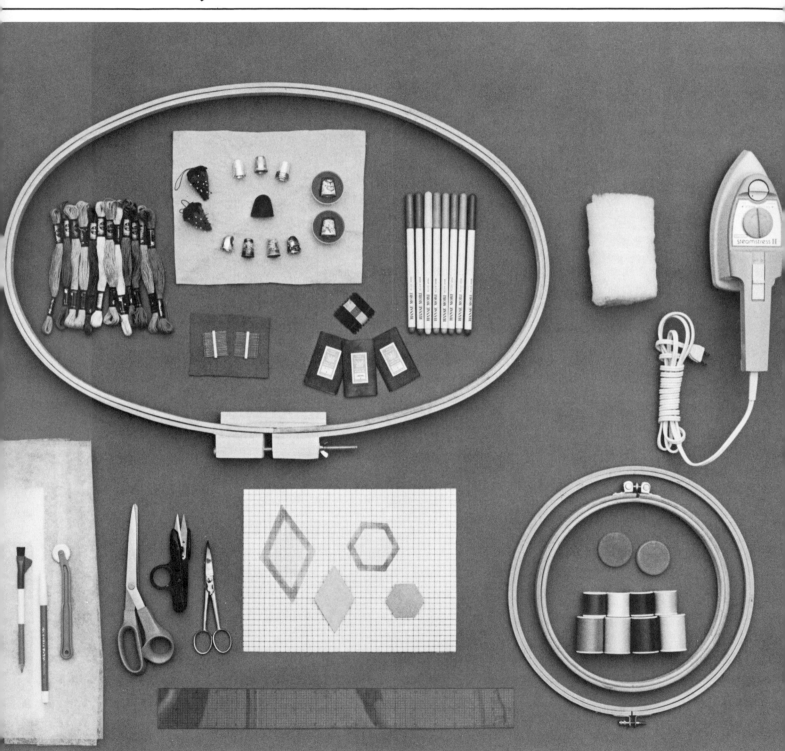

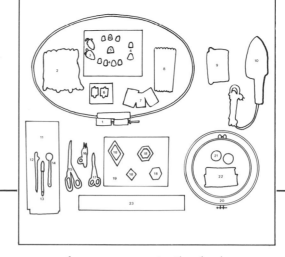

The following assortment of tools used in quilting projects is pictured on the opposite page. Suppliers are listed on page 216.

1 *Oval quilting hoop.*

2 *Cotton embroidery floss.*

3 *Pin cushions.*

4 *Thimbles.*

5 *Quilter's leather thimble:* to be worn on the forefinger of the hand under the frame.

6 *Quilting needles:* known as *Betweens,* size 8 are short and fine so that they slip easily through the fabric, but are strong enough to dive through three layers, prick the finger under the frame and come up again without bending.

7 *Embroidery needles.*

8 *Colored markers:* for designing.

9 *Polyester Batting:* in sheet form for use as interlining between quilt top and backing. Also available loose for padding appliqué, etc.

10 *Steam iron:* with a small sole plate, ideal for pressing small areas.

11 *Fusible interfacing:* thin pellon web for bonding two fabrics in appliqué. (Stitch Witchery, Wonder Under)

12 *Marking pencil:* one end for marking light-colored fabrics, the other for dark.

13 *Water-erasable marker:* for tracing quilt design on fabric.

14 *Tracing wheel.*

15 *Fabric scissors:* designed for left- or right-handed cutters.

16 *Thread snippers.*

17 *Curved scissors:* for easy cutting of circles or curved shapes.

18 *Metal templates:* hardwearing, will not lose their shape.

19 *Graph paper:* also "quadrille" paper, four squares to the inch.

20 *Round hoops:* medium and small for quilting small areas.

21 *Bee's wax:* makes thread stronger and reduces tangling. Quilting thread is ready-waxed.

22 *Quilting and sewing threads:* should be #50–#70.

23 *Clear plastic ruler.*

In addition to the basic tools, the following supplies will prove particularly useful.

Acetate: clear plastic film for templates. The edges do not roughen or wear down, however often they are used, and the desired area of a print can easily be seen through the acetate before the shape is cut.

Dressmaker's carbon: Used for transferring designs, available in all colors.

Erasable marker: the marker comes in a medium blue, which marks on dark and light–colored fabrics. It can be used to outline templates and delineate your quilting designs and patchwork or appliqué pieces. To remove the unnecessary lines, simply dampen the design with cold water and watch the lines disappear. Never forget and bundle the finished quilt into your washing machine; always remove the lines with cold water *first*. Hot water and/or certain detergents will "set" the blue lines and render them permanent.

Glass, round-headed pins: the round heads cause the thread to glance off the pins instead of wrapping itself around them as you hand stitch.

QUILTING TERMS

SELVAGE: The finished edge on either side of the width of fabric.

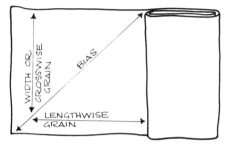

GRAIN: The fabric construction or weave, vertical (lengthwise grain) or horizontal (crosswise grain). A diagonal cut is called "bias."

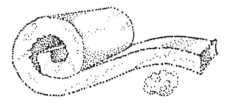

BATTING OR FILLER: The Dacron padding, blanket, or other material put between the backing and the quilt top to pad the quilt.

TEMPLATES: Brown paper, sandpaper, metal, or clear plastic pattern shapes for marking designs on fabric.

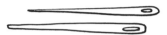

BETWEENS: Short, firm needles for quilting. Sizes 8 to 10 are good.

STAYSTITCHING: A line of stitching around the edge to hold the shape and prevent fraying, in appliqué.

APPLIQUÉ: Stitching one fabric in a cut-out design onto a background piece of fabric.

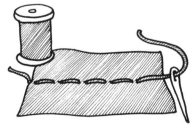

SELF-COLOR THREAD: Thread used for appliqué or embroidery that matches exactly the color of the background.

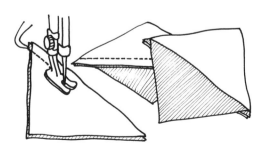

PIECING: Joining patchwork pieces to form a large area of material.

WHOLE-CLOTH QUILT: A quilt top made of a large, single piece of fabric.

BLOCK: The unit used to simplify construction of a quilt when it is not made of one whole piece of fabric. The entire area of the quilt may be divided into large squares or blocks, which are subdivided for patchwork or appliqué.

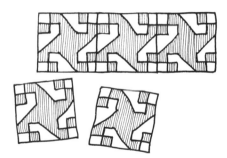

SETTING: Arranging and joining the pieced or appliquéd blocks together to form a quilt top.

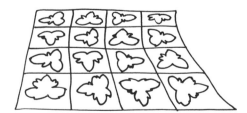

QUILT TOP OR FACE: The patchwork or appliqué top of the quilt that is ready for quilting or joining in some way to the "sandwich" formed by the backing and batting.

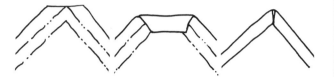

MITERING: Diagonal fold of corner edges to make a flat join at corners.

BORDER OR FRAME: A wide band around the edge of a quilt, usually part of the design.

SASHING: Wide strips of fabric stitched across the joins where the blocks meet.

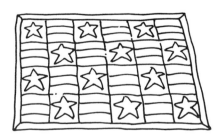

BINDING: A narrow, bias strip stitched around the edges of the quilt. It wears best if it is made of doubled fabric.

THEN, FRAMES

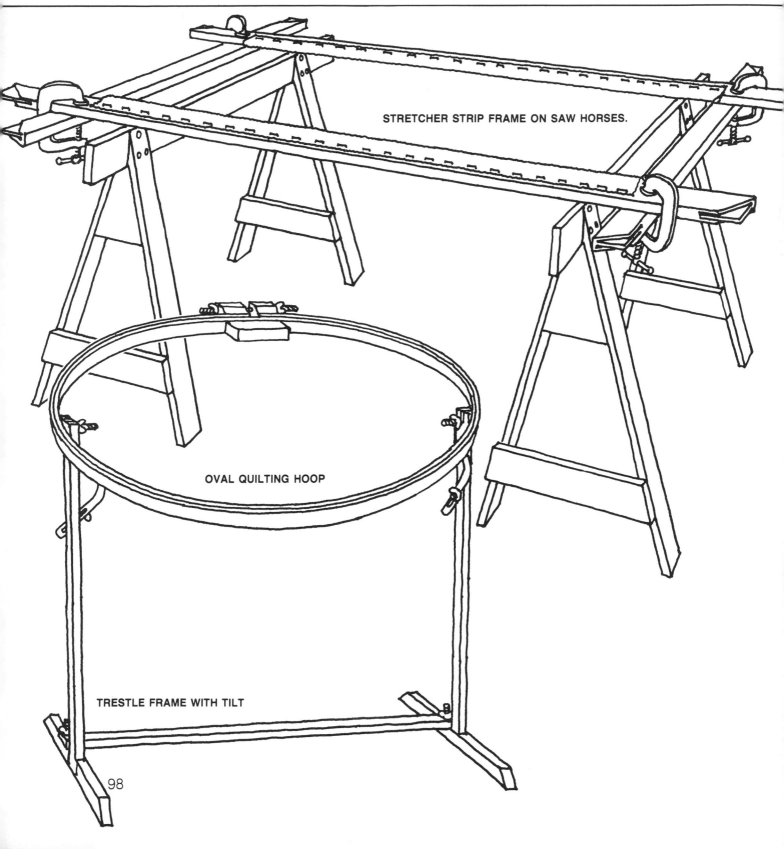

STRETCHER STRIP FRAME ON SAW HORSES.

OVAL QUILTING HOOP

TRESTLE FRAME WITH TILT

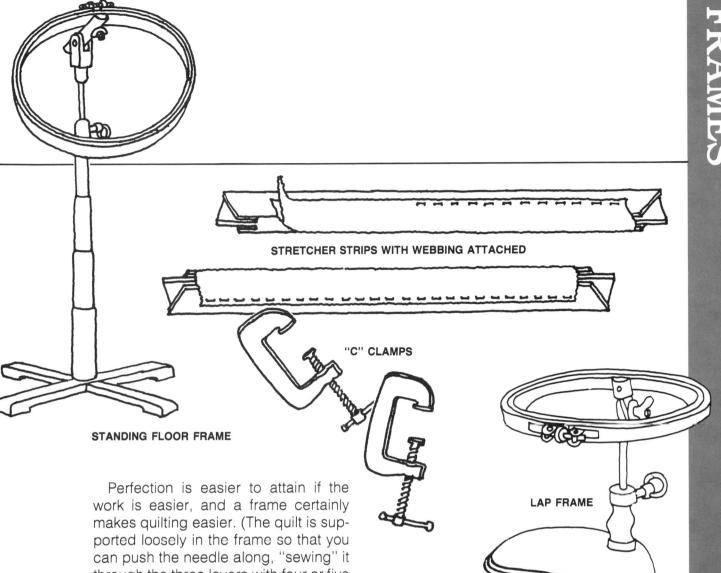

STRETCHER STRIPS WITH WEBBING ATTACHED

"C" CLAMPS

LAP FRAME

STANDING FLOOR FRAME

Perfection is easier to attain if the work is easier, and a frame certainly makes quilting easier. (The quilt is supported loosely in the frame so that you can push the needle along, "sewing" it through the three layers with four or five stitches on the needle at one time.)

A round hoop on a floor stand or lap base is ideal for quilting small blocks, and can be used for large quilts as well. For large quilts, however, an oval or square frame is best. The square frame has the advantage of creating a larger work area so that several quilters can work together.

If a square frame is not available, a good substitute is a set of artist's stretcher strips. These are sold in modules of one inch and are available in almost any size from an art supply store. With a heavy-duty staple gun, stretch webbing or doubled strips of ticking to one side of two of the longest stretcher strips. Following the steps on pages 102-103, attach the opposite ends of your quilt to this webbing and roll up the quilt on both sides, leaving the amount you need exposed, for the quilting to begin, in the center. Then, with two more stretcher strips, four "C" clamps, and some tape, you can stretch the quilt out square and rest it on saw horses for working. The drawing of this on the opposite page has been left without a quilt in the frame for clarity. A support stand with adjustable tilt is lighter and more convenient than saw horses; an instructional drawing of this is shown on the next page.

MAKING YOUR OWN FRAME

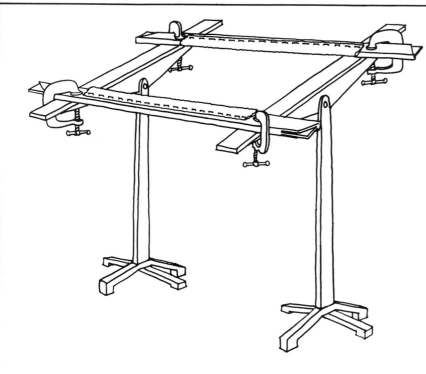

MATERIALS
- ½″ maple or sugar pine stock for top horizontal (A).
- ⅜″ maple or sugar pine stock for top vertical (B).
- 1″ maple or sugar pine stock for vertical and base (C, D, and E).
- 1¾″ carriage bolt with two ¼″ lock washers and one wing nut for top assembly
- 3¼″ carriage bolt with one ¼″ lock washer and one wing nut for bottom of base.
- Two 3″ slotted wood screws for base assembly.
- White household glue or tightbond glue for base and top assembly.
- Sandpaper, medium and smooth for sanding finished pieces.
- Varnish, shellac, or wax.

TOOLS
Bandsaw or sabersaw, drill, screwdriver.

ASSEMBLY
Cut wood to specified size with a bandsaw or sabersaw. Cut out groove in top of vertical piece (C) so that it will receive the head of tressle piece (B). Be sure to leave a small triangle of wood intact so that the head adjusts properly (shown by broken lines in the diagram). Drill holes for carriage bolts and screws.

Apply glue to top pieces (A) and (B); clamp together and let dry.

Countersink carriage bolt into base piece (D). Apply glue to it and vertical piece (C) and screw together tightly. Sand all pieces until smooth. Apply finish. Rub or sand lightly until smooth. Assemble adjustable pieces and voilà!

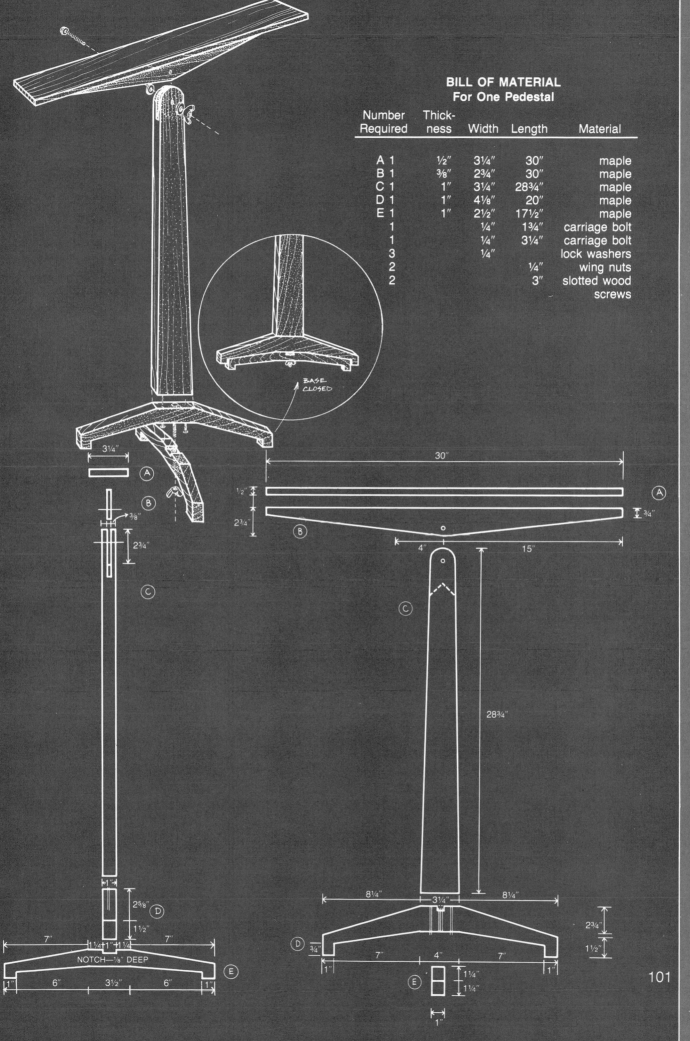

BILL OF MATERIAL
For One Pedestal

Number Required	Thick-ness	Width	Length	Material
A 1	½"	3¼"	30"	maple
B 1	⅜"	2¾"	30"	maple
C 1	1"	3¼"	28¾"	maple
D 1	1"	4⅛"	20"	maple
E 1	1"	2½"	17½"	maple
1		¼"	1¾"	carriage bolt
1		¼"	3¼"	carriage bolt
3		¼"		lock washers
2			¼"	wing nuts
2			3"	slotted wood screws

BASE CLOSED

MOUNTING THE QUILT IN A SQUARE FRAME

First, cut your lining 4 inches larger than your quilt top. Then attach your quilt (lining first) to the stretcher strips. For this you will need pins, tape, heavy-duty thread, and a pencil. Make sure your stretcher strips project a good six to eight inches on either side of your quilt lining, leaving room for attaching the "C" clamps. Mark the midpoint on your webbing and one side of your quilt lining and pin them together with the lining face down.

Place one pin straight down in the

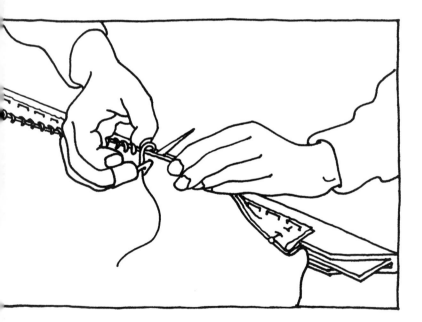

center of one side, stretch the lining tight, and hold it with one pin at each end, as shown. Starting in the center, oversew the lining to the webbing, working out to one side. Start again in the center and oversew out to the other side. Repeat this at the opposite end. This will ensure that your quilt is lined up evenly, ready for stretching.

Now lay the stretchers and lining flat

on the floor or a table and carefully smooth the batting or padding on top, as shown. If the batting is in two or more pieces, overlap at least 1½ inches at the joins.

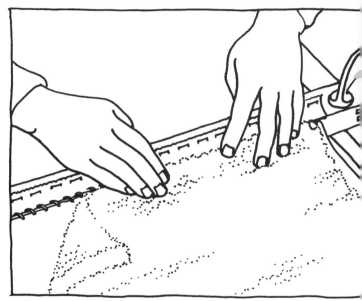

Lay your quilt top over the batting, right side up. Be sure your patchwork top is even and smooth. Baste all three layers together, as shown, with the special broad basting stitch that will hold the layers together as though they were one (see Quilting, page 110). Instead of starting the basting from one end, some people prefer to mark the center of the quilt top and batting. Pin the three layers together and baste from the center, radiating the lines of basting from the center point out to the sides. Others baste a straight line across the quilt an inch or so in from the edge, and then "needle" lines of basting across the quilt at wide intervals, as shown.

Once the basting is complete, roll up the quilt on the stretchers, leaving the

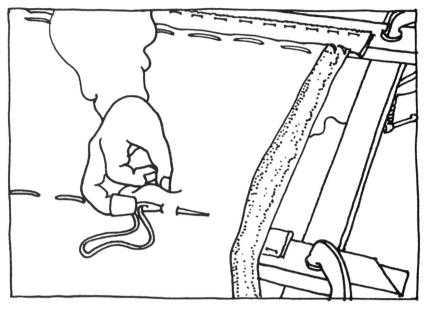

part you need exposed for the quilting to begin. To stretch the quilt in the width, pin seam binding tape or strips of scrap fabric along either side as shown, wrapping it over the side bars to hold it firmly.

Depending on the design, it is often easier to begin quilting in the center and work out to either side. The design also determines whether you mark out your quilting patterns with templates as you go, or whether you mark the whole design before basting the quilt top to the frame. Cutting templates and transferring the quilting designs to your quilt top is shown on the next few pages.

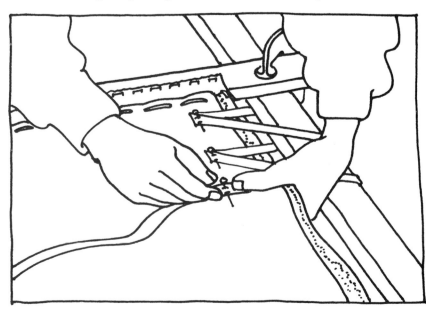

Traditional designs for quilting, such as feathers and round-petalled flowers, may be traced from the following pages. You can experiment with many different quilting designs, as long as they balance the design of your quilt. Your quilting pattern should have smooth flowing lines with wide spaces in between to allow the quilt to puff between the lines of stitches. Look at the quilted border of land, sea, and sky surrounding the prizewinning quilt Leda on page 74.

To make a template for your quilting

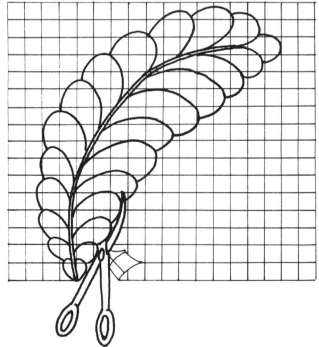

design, draw your shapes on graph paper, glue the paper to cardboard, and cut out the designs, as shown. You need not cut in every line on your template. A basic outline is often enough to guide your stitches, and you can fill in any small areas freehand. For example,

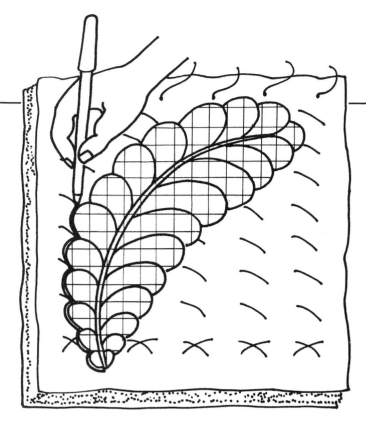

once the outline and the center vein of a feather are cut and stencilled, it is easy to stitch any branching veins freehand. A sharp knife is ideal for cutting

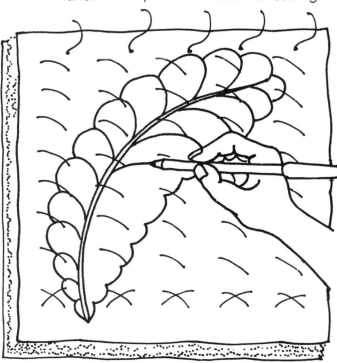

areas that are impossible to reach with scissors, such as center veins of feathers and center circles of flowers. Work on a hard, protected surface as you cut, and leave a small, uncut "bridge" of cardboard here and there to hold the separate sections of the template together.

Position the quilting template on the quilt top and outline around the design with a marker or tailor's chalk as shown. Using an erasable marker, tailor's chalk, or even indenting the design into the fabric with the point of the needle also gives you the freedom of drawing designs without templates.

If you want to transfer a fairly complex design instead of a repeat pattern, you can transfer it with dressmaker's carbon in the following manner: lay the fabric on a hard surface, face up; then lay the carbon on top, face down. Position the design on top of the carbon and hold everything in place with heavy weights (books are good). Trace the design by running the tracing wheel firmly along the outlines, frequently lifting a corner of the paper to make sure that the design is transferring to the fabric with a clear dotted line. Use pale blue carbon paper for transferring designs onto light-colored fabrics, white carbon paper on dark fabrics. Unwanted small dots should wash out easily afterwards. *Always* test your carbon paper on a piece of scrap fabric before marking on your quilt top, to be sure it will wash out easily and completely.

BASICS OF QUILTING

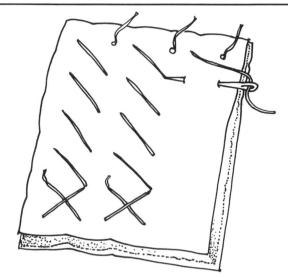

Detail of My Garden Quilt, shown on page 72, made by Walla Doleski, Michigan.

Before you can begin quilting, you must baste the three layers of your quilt together. The broad basting stitch is ideal for this; it holds all the fabrics together as though they were one. Knot the thread, and starting at the top left, work down to the bottom of your quilt, taking a series of evenly spaced horizontal stitches. At the bottom, go back and form a cross stitch to secure the thread. Cover the entire area of your quilt in this way, spacing the rows about 2 inches apart. Next, mount the

quilt into a frame—square or oval if you are quilting the entire top, round if you are doing apartment quilting (as shown opposite). Do not stretch the layers too tightly; leave the quilt slightly slack in the frame.

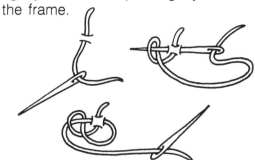

Begin with a quilter's knot, shown here, or bury a small knot in the batting by pulling the thread until the knot "pops" between the layers, as shown.

The quilting stitch is simply a running stitch that will become beautifully even with practice. With one hand on top and

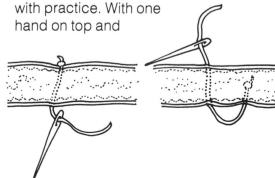

110

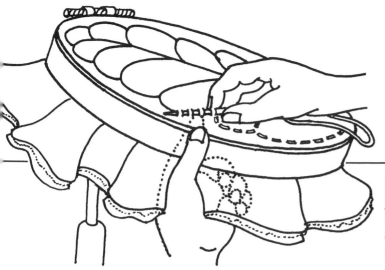

the other underneath, push the needle straight down through all three layers, prick the finger underneath (just to make sure you are there) and return the needle to the top. Continue, taking as many stitches as you can get easily on the needle. (You will take more as you gain experience and increase speed and rhythm.) Each stitch length should be equal to the space between the stitches, and the stitches should be of equal length on either side of the quilt. Some quilters like to feel the needle as it comes through, others protect their fingers with a leather thimble (see Tools, page 94) or tape. Try to train yourself to be able to use either hand on top; this makes it simpler to work in different directions. To end, knot the thread, take the last stitch, and "pop" the knot into the batting. Run the needle through the batting a few inches before cutting the thread.

If you are doing apartment quilting

(quilting each entire block before it is joined to another), you should leave 2 inches of fabric unquilted all around the edge of the block so that you can make neat joins afterwards. To quilt by machine, first stretch the block with the quilting design marked in a small round hoop. Remove the presser foot. The thickness of the hoop should be on top, as shown, so that the fabric can lie flat against the base of the machine.

Joining can be done by first seaming right sides of the blocks together as shown in the diagram, below left. Then blindstitch the seams together on the reverse side as shown, below right. To work the blind stitch, slide the needle through the fold, parallel to the seam. Go straight across and repeat, taking a flat, shallow stitch on the other side of the seam, as shown. As you stitch, pull the stitches firmly and they become invisible, hence the name blind stitch.

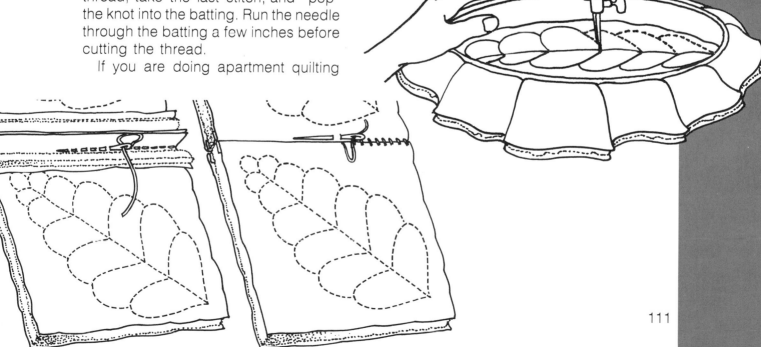

BACKGROUND QUILTING

Detail of Ray of Light quilt, shown on pages 46-47, made by Jinny Beyer, Virginia.

Detail of Camellia Cameo, shown on page 77, made by Annie Sellers Davis, Alabama.

Any of the preceding quilting patterns can be used alone, as can any of the background patterns shown here. But the combination of an open design, such as a feather, with a background of bunched quilting, is very attractive.

The interlocking circles pattern is made by drawing around a wine glass. Keep the first row straight by securing a yardstick to the fabric with masking tape and holding the wine glass beside it. With practice, your lines will be straight and even. The shell pattern, or Mother of Thousands, is done in the same way, but by tracing around only half the wine glass, fitting the curves together like bricks.

The grid pattern can be made easily with a yardstick if the width of the yardstick is the same as the space desired between the rows. Rule the first line beside the yardstick, flip it over, and rule the next line parallel to the first. When all the lines have been marked in one direction, turn the yardstick and mark lines in the other direction. Masking tape is another way to mark grid patterns: *Lightly* put down one length of tape at a time and quilt beside the tape.

Another method of marking straight lines for quilting is to rub chalk on a string, stretch the string taut between two pins, then pull upwards and "snap" the string back onto the cloth. The chalk will fall on the fabric in a straight line. Use dark chalk for light-colored fabrics, light chalk on dark fabrics.

Contour quilting simply follows the shape of the outline of your appliqué or patchwork, row after row. If you feel unequal to the task of keeping the rows even, you can rule a grid to guide your spacing. Most quilters prefer the hand-done look of patterns marked out by eye.

Bunched or meandering quilting, which is time consuming but beautiful, is done by working rows of contour quilting very close together. Because the rows are so close, an entirely different effect results.

INTERLOCKING CIRCLES

GRID

BUNCHED

CONTOUR

SHELL

TRAPUNTO

Detail of baby quilt, shown on page 19, circa 1825. America Hurrah Antiques.

Trapunto is a kind of "super padding" that can be added to a quilt to make certain areas stand out in high relief. This shows to most advantage on a "whole-cloth" quilt in white on white, such as the one shown here and on page 19. It can also be beautifully combined with padded appliqué as on page 25.

Begin by basting a muslin backing with the design traced on it to the reverse side of the finished but unquilted top. (Use the "quilt basting" stitch shown on page 110.) Then, working

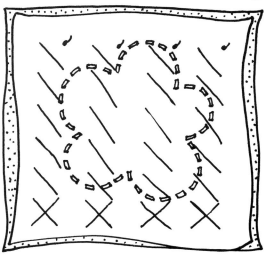

from the reverse side and following the pattern, outline the design with a running stitch. Or instead of working a running stitch, the design may be outlined in backstitch, resulting in a bold line that clearly delineates the pattern. To outline the design in backstitch, you must actually work the stem stitch on

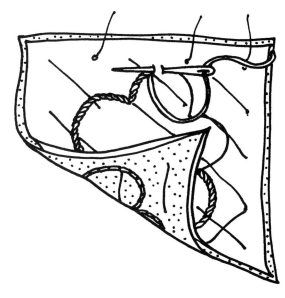

114

the reverse side. This results in back-stitch on the right side, as shown. When the stitching is complete, remove the basting and cut slits in the muslin. To avoid cutting the fabric of the quilt when making the initial slit in the muslin, separate the muslin from the quilt top with two crossed pins, as shown. The

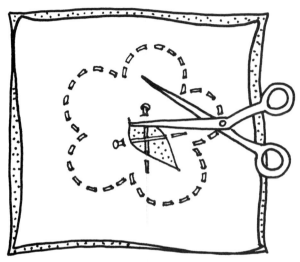

tips of the scissors will then glance off the pins, cutting only the muslin back-ing. Push in the batting with the tips of scissors, padding the shape lightly but

firmly. Finally, sew up the slits in the backing. When stuffing, do not pack the batting in so tightly that the shape becomes hard and rigid, but do make sure that batting is pushed evenly into the corners and narrow points of the design.

To do trapunto by machine, baste the muslin to the quilt top and mount it in an embroidery hoop. The thickness of the frame should be on top so that the stretched fabric lies flat against the base of the machine with the muslin on top. Remove the presser foot so that you can maneuver the frame to stitch in any direction. Once you get used to the idea that the needle remains stationary while the design in the hoop is moved to keep the needle on the line, you will be able to gain control and increase your speed. Once the design is out-lined by machine stitching, proceed with the stuffing as described for tra-punto by hand.

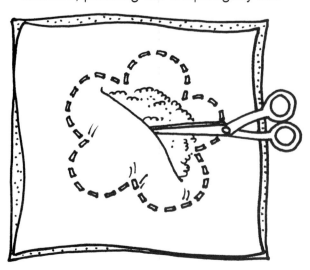

Detail of a silk jacket made by the author.

Both trapunto and Italian trapunto are padded after the stitching is done, instead of before. The Italian, or channel quilting (also called corded quilting) is most suited to designs with narrow bands, such as the ones on this and the next two pages, because the padding is done with a needle threaded with thick wool. Channel quilting makes excellent border designs, and it can be attractively combined with a background of all-over quilting.

Follow the same procedure outlined on the preceding two pages for trapunto, using a running stitch to outline the design. When stitching is complete,

remove the basting. Then, using a large blunt needle and a doubled thread of bulky knitting yarn (or a single strand of any thick, yet lightweight Dacron mixture), run through the channels as shown in the diagram. Make each stitch as long as is comfortable on the needle, pull through, and return again to the same hole to continue. But instead of pulling the wool flat at the "exit" points, leave a little "bump" as shown, to allow for stretch in wear and shrinkage in wash. This will ensure that your channels will not become puckered by too tight a padding. For the same reason, as you pad, pull the fabric on the bias this way and that to take up the maximum amount of yarn in the channel. If all-over quilting is combined with Italian trapunto, it should be done as the final step after all the channel quilting is complete.

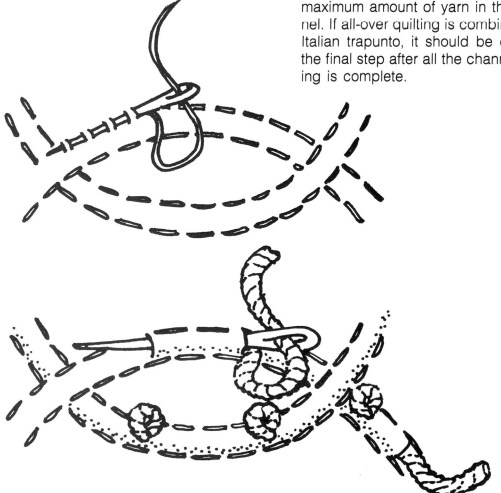

118

TUFTING

Detail of Winner's Circle quilt, shown on pages 52-53, made by Yukon Norman, Utah.

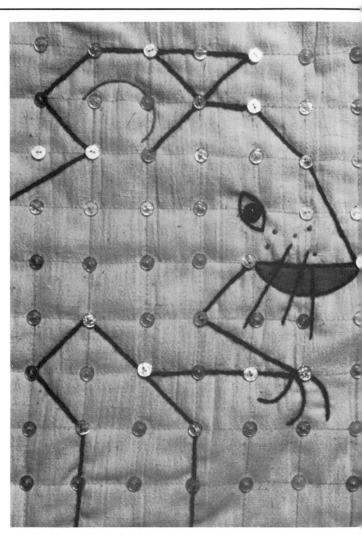

Detail of Draw Me quilt, shown on pages 48-49, made by Linae Frei, New York.

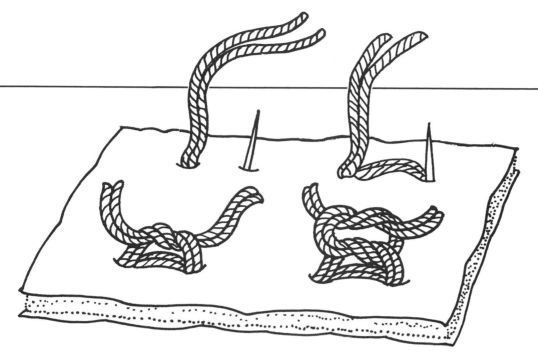

Tufting is an excellent way of holding the layers of a quilt together without stitching. Thread a chenille needle (a long-eyed needle with a sharp point) with heavy embroidery floss or knitting worsted. Starting on top, push the needle straight through all three layers of your quilt, leaving a 4-inch tag end on top. Come up, go down again in the same hole as the first stitch, and come up once more, as shown. Tie the two tag ends together in a square knot: right over left, left over right. Snip the ends evenly to the desired length.

Space your knots in straight rows or in "brick" fashion over the entire quilt top as desired. Tufting may also be done with buttons, as shown. Prizewinning examples of tufting are the Winner's Circle quilt on pages 52-53 and Draw Me on pages 48-49. The button spacing on the latter was determined by first machine-stitching a "grid" over the quilt top. The three quilt layers were then basted together and the butttons stitched down at each intersection of the grid lines.

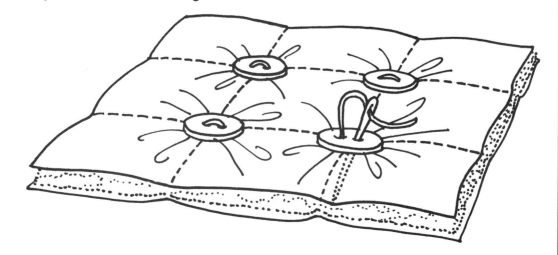

Detail of Autumn Leaves quilt, shown on page 68, made by Karen Hagen, West Virginia.

Appliqué is the technique of stitching one fabric to another. The applied shapes should lie flat and smooth without bubbles or wrinkles; in fact, the two materials should become as one. This is most easily accomplished if you follow three important guidelines: 1) work in an embroidery frame; 2) select 100% cotton fabric so that the turnbacks will be easy to handle and will not spring back and behave badly; and 3) always

cut the fabrics so that the grain of the appliquéd piece will run in the same direction as the grain of the background fabric once the two are stitched together.

Begin by marking the outlines of the leaf shapes on the appliqué fabric. Position the shapes on the fabric, as shown, at exactly the same angle they will ultimately be when they are applied to the background fabric. In this way,

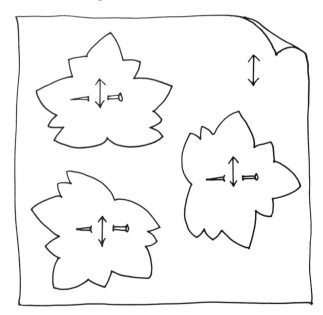

the two fabrics will have the same "pull."

Cut out each leaf shape, leaving ¼-inch turnbacks. Outline each shape with staystitching ¼ inch in from the edge. Clip curves, turn, press, and baste turnbacks to the wrong side of the fabric, as shown. Pin each leaf in position on the background fabric; then sew the leaf down with tiny stitches

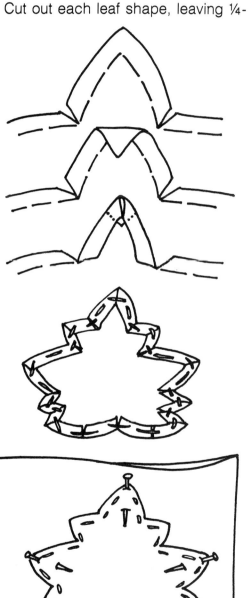

made at right angles to the edges, as shown. With small shapes, it may be easier to pin them in position without preparing the turnbacks, then fold under the turnbacks with your needle to make a smooth clear outline, stitching it down as you go.

To appliqué by machine, lay a square of fabric with the design drawn on it, down on the background fabric, right sides up, matching the grains. Outline with straight machine stitching, then cut away the excess fabric around the appliqué design. Finally, outline with satin stitch and trim any loose ends. Complex designs to be appliquéd by machine may be easily done from the reverse side (see page 206).

Detail of Quilted Montage, shown on page 80, made by Caroline Riddle, Tennessee.

have chosen for that area, trace around the shape, and cut it out, leaving a generous seam allowance all around. You will then be able to stitch each piece in its correct position on the muslin backing.

Start with the area that is visually behind all the others (in this case, the sky). Overlay the lower edge of the sky with the first hill, then overlay that with the next hill, and so on until you come to the final top layers.

Where the edge of one layer is covered by another, the hidden edge should be left flat, without turnbacks, to avoid unnecessary bulk. In fact, the hidden edges that will be covered by another layer need not even be cut to shape.

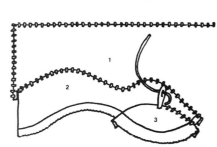

To "build" a picture in fabric, begin with an outline drawing on paper. From this, trace the outline on muslin as a base for your appliqué. Next, piece by piece, cut the pattern shapes out of paper. Position each shape on the straight grain of the appliqué fabric you

Embroidery details, such as the fish in the river and the barn door, should be stitched on the fabric before it is cut out and applied. Finally, backing and batting are basted to the back of the appliquéd quilt top, or "picture," and the shapes are outlined with quilting, as shown in the photograph.

LAYERED APPLIQUÉ

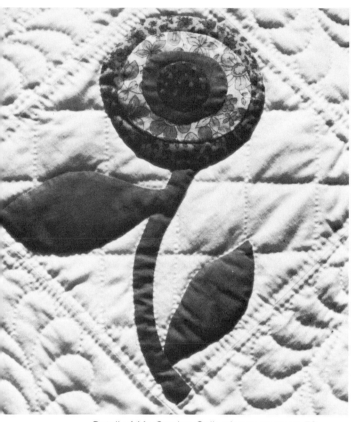

Detail of My Garden Quilt, shown on page 72, made by Walla Doleski, Michigan.

curved scissors, cut out the top circle, leaving ¼-inch turnbacks as shown. Staystitch around the circle ¼ inch from the edge. Clip the curves, press, and baste the turnbacks to the wrong side of the fabric.

Pin this circle to the next layer of fabric (which is square—not cut to

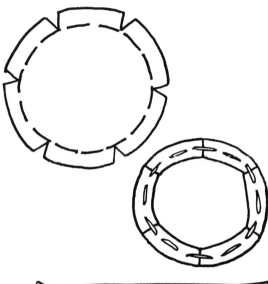

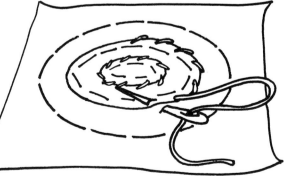

In the appliquéd flower design shown here, the blossom is made of circles laid one on top of the other. Start with the uppermost layer first. With

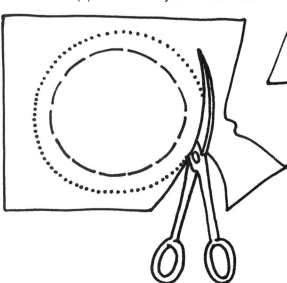

shape yet) and hemstitch the top circle in place using matching thread, a fine needle, and taking tiny invisible stitches. Then cut and baste the next layer, as the first. Repeat for the bottom and final circle.

125

Deborah Kakalia shown with examples of her Hawaiian quilts. Courtesy of Family Circle.

The lovely Pikake and Tuberose quilt on page 83 is typical of the patterns originating in Hawaii. When the missionaries took quilting and patchwork to Hawaii in the 1800s, it quickly became popular, but not at all in the way the New England women who taught it had envisioned. The missionaries started by teaching the Islanders to fold paper as a basic structure for geometric patchwork piecing, so that small shapes could be joined from the left-over scraps of clothing fabric. But the

Hawaiians wore no clothes and so had no leftover remnants to join! Instead, they had large pieces of fine tapa cloth made for bedding from the inside bark of a tree. The story behind their unique designs is that one young pupil noticed the shadow of a palm tree, quickly cut the design out of folded paper, and then and there the unique Hawaiian quilt was born. The patterns are usually in two contrasting colors and are quilted with contour lines suggestive of the ripples of the Pacific Ocean.

Begin by making a small scale paper pattern to see how your final design will look. Cut an 8-inch square out of drawing or graph paper. Fold it in half and in half again to form a 4-inch square, four thicknesses thick. Fold this small square diagonally as shown. If you open it up now, you will see eight segments radiating from the center.

Fold the paper up again and, *holding the center point of the triangle towards you* (marked with a dot in the diagram), sketch a simple design such as a palm tree. Draw one-half of the tree on one edge, one-half along the other edge, and a simple, smaller tree in the center. Cut out the design. Open up the pattern, and if you feel it needs to be more lacy, refold and snip again. Once the

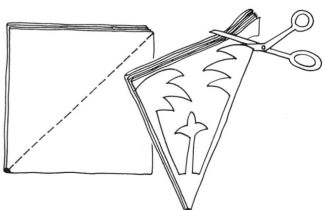

design is to your liking, you are ready to make the full-scale pattern.

The measurements given are for a 90-inch square design that will fit a standard-sized double bed; a similar procedure will work for any size design. For the full-scale pattern, fold a 45-inch square of heavy wrapping paper once diagonally, copy the design from the small folded pattern onto the wrapping paper—proportionately larger—and cut it out. (All eight layers are not needed in the full-scale pattern.) Unfold it to be sure that all is well, then refold it.

Fold a 90-inch square of fabric very carefully, *just as you folded the original small paper pattern.* Lay the folded, full-scale pattern on the folded cloth, pinning it securely in many places. Cut all eight layers of cloth at once, following the pattern lines and leaving a ⅛- to ¼-inch turnback around the design. When opened, the entire design is in one piece, ready to appliqué.

To make a border or a pattern with a design that hangs from the border, hold the center point of the small folded paper square (again marked with a dot) towards you. Cut the folded paper right across about one-third above the center point. (From this one-third a small central design may be cut.) On the folded two-thirds remaining, cut a de-

sign *along the eight raw edges* as shown, which will form a border when it is opened up. Make a full-scale pattern and use it to cut the fabric, following the same procedure outlined for the central appliqué design.

To appliqué the design to your background fabric, first crease or baste

lines through the center of your background fabric in both directions. Then stretch it flat on the floor, holding it with masking tape. Unfold the appliqué design and pin it down firmly, matching the center lines and being very careful not to stretch it out of shape. After carefully basting the appliqué design to the background, the quilt top can be mounted into a square frame (see Frames, page 102), and appliquéd. Start appliquéing in the center to keep the design from "creeping." Clip the curves and turn under the ⅛- to ¼-inch turnbacks with your needle and stitch the appliqué down (see Appliqué, page 122). Quilt with contour quilting (see Background Quilting, page 112), spacing the rows about ½ inch apart.

DESIGNING PATCHWORK

However complex a geometric pieced design may appear, a little experience shows you that the basic construction is extremely simple. The technique is based on folded paper. American pioneers may not have had much in the way of drafting tools, but they knew that even a piece of newspaper or an old letter could easily be folded to form a perfect square. The paper could be folded again and refolded to make pattern pieces that could multiply as quickly as shaking a kaleidoscope—with the same surprise factor at seeing the multiples appear.

The first step in designing patchwork is to measure the bed for which the quilt is to be made. Once the size is determined, divide the entire area into large blocks of equal size. Then subdivide each block into smaller squares, which can be used as the framework for an unlimited variety of patchwork patterns. Depending on the design you will construct, these small squares can be in odd or even numbers.

The simplest way to begin designing is to fold your block in half and in half again, resulting in four squares. This simple patchwork pattern is known as Four Patch. (It can also be divided into multiples of four.) If you fold your square into thirds in both directions and open it up, you will have nine small squares, a pattern known as Nine Patch. (This can also be subdivided into thirty-six squares.) If, however, you fold your square into fifths, you will have twenty-five squares. For the sake of simplicity, this pattern is called Five Patch; following the same rule, forty-nine squares is called Seven Patch.

These grids of folds make it easy to develop seemingly complex patterns. By simply dividing one square into two triangles, or joining two squares together to make a rectangle, or adding circles drawn around a thread spool or an egg cup, you can achieve a wide

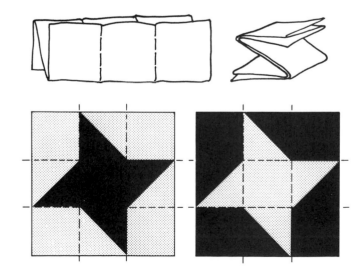

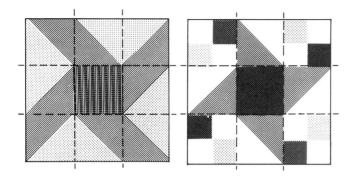

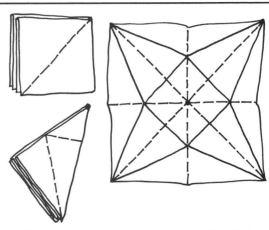

range of geometric designs. The design possibilities become limitless when you add color.

A simple star can be made by folding a square in half and in half again. Then, *holding the center point towards you* (mark it with a dot, to be sure), fold diagonally in half, right to left; then fold again right to left, as shown by the dotted lines in the diagram. Fold over the tip as shown, open out the paper pattern, and you will have a perfectly balanced star shape.

A hexagon can be made by folding a circle in half and then in thirds, as shown. The easiest way to fold the circle accurately is to fold it in half, and then to curve it as though you were making a paper cup. When the two opposite edges are evenly spaced, smooth it flat, being careful to pinch the point firmly to crease it precisely at the center. Cut a straight edge across the curves opposite the point, as shown, and the result is a perfect hexagon shape.

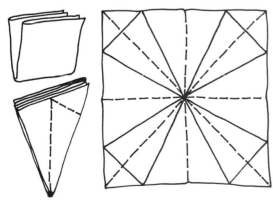

To make a pointed star, take another square of paper and fold just as you did for the simple star, but instead of holding the *center* point, make your folds while *holding the point opposite the center point*. The result is a four-pointed star with a central square.

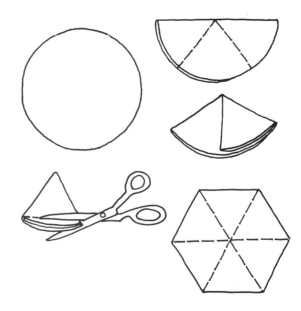

SETTING THE BLOCKS

Once the blocks are designed, the next step is to set them together and decide on the color scheme. So that your quilt will "read" well, you must decide on which areas are to be dark, and which are to be light colored. Draw your blocks on graph paper, filling in the dark areas with pencil and leaving the light areas blank. Quadrille paper (bold scale graph paper) is a help in estimating the size and scale of the

blocks. Then you can cut out, arrange, and rearrange the blocks until you find a "set" that takes your fancy. The diagrams illustrate how the same pattern can look completely different, depending on how it is arranged.

ESTIMATING YARDAGE

Once you've settled on the basic geometrics and the color scheme of your pattern, you must establish the size of your quilt and calculate how much fabric you will need. Measure your mattress, allowing for the "tuck" under the pillow and the "drop" (fabric on three sides that "drops" from the top of the bed to the dust ruffle or to the floor).

Divide the quilt area into equal squares, with 1 inch equal to one

square on your graph paper. If your quilt is to be an overall design with, say, a center medallion, it is a good idea to have the size outlined on graph paper so that you can establish the center, mark out the diagonals, and map out proportions of general areas on this small scale first.

An easy way to estimate yardage for a quilt is to cut out your pieces in actual size for one block of your quilt. Arrange all the pieces that are the same color so that there is plenty of fabric between each for turnbacks. Then measure the area they take up. Multiply that area by the number of times that particular block will repeat, to calculate how much of each color you will need.

Alternatively, if you are unsure of your arithmetic, cut a paper pattern for *every* piece of *each* color that will make up your quilt. Lay out all the pieces of one color on 36-inch-wide shelf paper, allowing space for turnbacks between each piece, and then measure the yardage they take up.

TIPS

• Cut templates for hand piecing *without* turnbacks. Trace around the template to get the exact stitching line, and cut ¼ inch beyond that line freehand for turnbacks.

• Cut all templates for machine piecing *with* seam allowances. You can then keep the pressure foot on the outer edge of the fabric, using this as a guide for keeping the seams accurate.

• For a triangle, never cut a square in fabric, and then cut it in half; it is difficult to get accurate seam allowances. Cut a triangle template first out of paper; then cut the shape out of fabric.

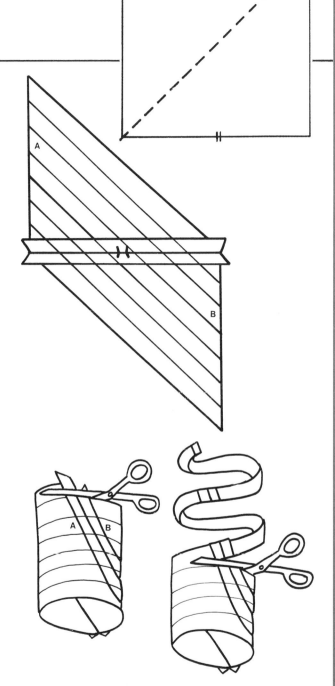

• Always piece one block before cutting the fabric shapes for a whole quilt, to see if your colors and shapes are accurate.

• Never try to "fit" a square into an angled corner made up of three squares that are already joined. Whenever possible, join your squares in straight rows within each block; then join the blocks in strips, and finally join the strips to form the quilt.

• For strength, do not press seams open; press them alternately to one side or the other.

• Press each block after it is finished, pressing dark seams away from light areas so that the color will not show through.

• Finish quilt edges with double bias binding, since the edge always receives the most wear. Cutting continuous bias strips saves time.

CONTINUOUS BIAS— CUTTING THE QUICK WAY

(1) On a large square of fabric (1 yard, 36 inches wide, for instance), mark the center of the width on each side. Cut the fabric in half diagonally, as shown.

(2) Join the two triangles, matching the points you marked before cutting. Using tailor's chalk, rule parallel lines across the longest length at approximately 2- to 4-inch intervals (depending upon the width you want the binding to be), as shown.

(3) Seam the two opposite sides (A & B) together to form a sleeve, as shown. Make sure one edge projects above the other at the seam by one width, as shown, and that the other markings match and run straight across the

seam. Also make sure that the raw edges of both the first seam and the sleeve seam are on the same side.

(4) Proceed to cut around along the chalked lines to form one continous bias strip (rather like peeling an apple).

HEXAGONS

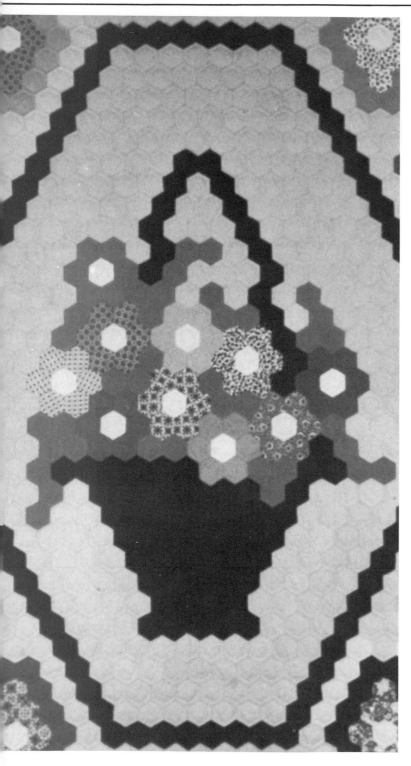

Patchwork can be pattern within pattern, forming the most intricate of patterns, or it can be simply formed by the shape itself, whether it is a square, a circle, or a hexagon. The hexagon shape is often used to form a flower. In the prizewinning quilt from Nebraska, Wanda Dawson made a flower basket surrounded by flower heads, a new twist on the traditional pattern known as Grandma's Flower Garden. The pattern for her design is on page 170.

Patchwork pieces with curved edges or awkward corners, such as a hexagon, are sure to be more accurate when pieced by hand, using paper patterns that are basted to each fabric shape. The paper can be left in until the entire quilt is finished, or removed and used over again. In some old quilts, the paper was never removed; it kept the quilt firm and added to the warmth!

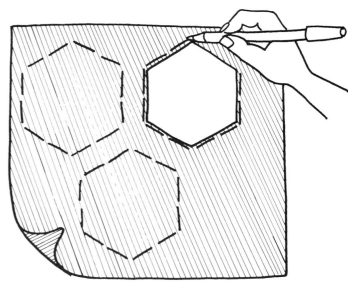

Detail of Grandma's Basket of Flowers, shown on pages 50-51, made by Wanda Dawson, Nebraska.

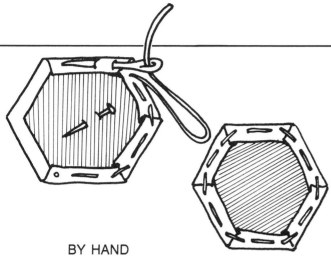

BY MACHINE

1) Cut out hexagon shapes from fabric. Sew two together, right sides facing, with a straight line of machine stitching. For ease of stitching, sew several pairs together with one line of stitching, as shown.

BY HAND

1) Cut a master pattern template or buy a metal or plastic template.

2) Cut out hexagon shapes from paper and pin the paper patterns to the wrong side of your fabric. Cut out, leaving ¼-inch turnbacks all around.

3) Fold and press turnbacks against the paper pattern; then baste them down all around.

4) Oversew the first pair together, right sides facing.

5) Sew hexagons together in groups of three, then join groups.

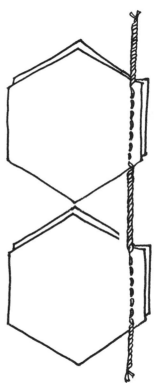

2) Stitch the remaining sides of each hexagon pair to other pairs of hexagons.

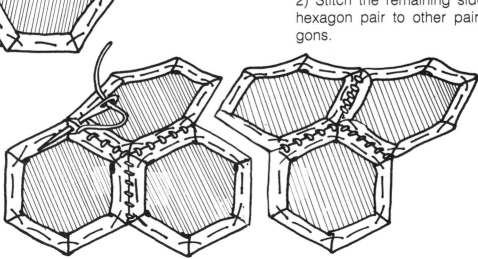

YO-YOS

Yo-Yos are circles of gathered fabric that create a marvelous three-dimensional effect. Making the Yo-Yos calls for extreme accuracy, for if each circle is not exactly the same size, joining the circles together will be impossible.

Begin by making a cardboard template exactly twice the size you want your finished circle to be. From this, trace and cut out brown paper templates which you will use as patterns for cutting your fabric. For perfect curves, cut out the paper patterns and the fabric shapes with curved scissors.

Follow the diagram, turning the fabric over the paper pattern and running a row of tiny stitches close to the edge.

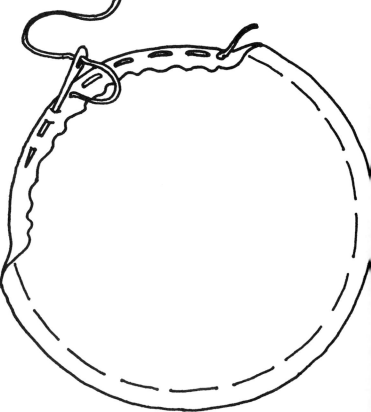

Pull out the paper pattern and draw the running stitches up tightly. Secure the thread firmly and press the gathered circle of fabric flat.

Join the circles together in strips or blocks in the desired color sequence by holding the circles together, right sides facing, and taking several over-sewing stitches close together.

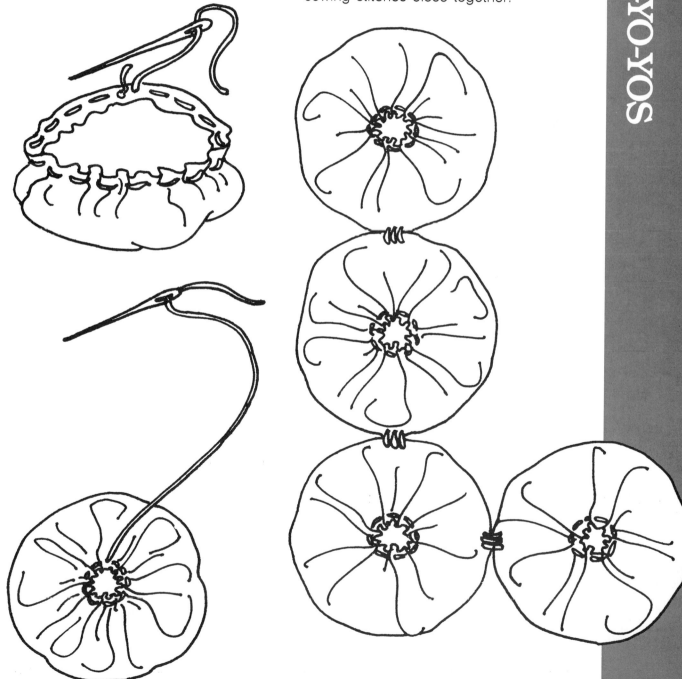

CATHEDRAL WINDOW

Cathedral Window, with its intriguing three-dimensional effect, requires no batting, no quilting, and no quilting frame. You can make it with light fabric for the folded squares and a dark material for the "windows," or vice versa. Lovely variations of this pattern can be made when you counterchange the lights and darks or printed and plain fabrics.

The size you make each square will depend on where you want to use the finished design, but it is important to know that the size of the final square will be only one-half the size of the first one because of the folding involved. (An 8-inch square will become a 4-inch square, for instance.)

Begin by making a square cardboard or sandpaper template pattern (8 inches square is a convenient size). Trace around the pattern on the straight grain of the fabric and cut it out with ½-inch turnbacks all around. Press the turnbacks to the wrong side of the fabric square as shown. Fold the square in half, wrong sides facing, and blind-

stitch the edges together halfway along both short sides, as shown in the diagram.

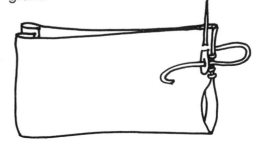

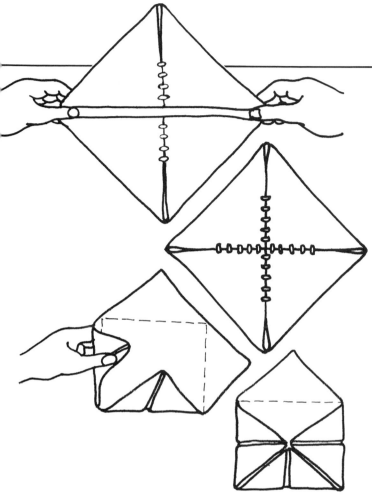

Cut a 3-inch square of contrasting material, press ½-inch turnbacks to the wrong side of the fabric, and position it in the center diamond, as shown. Roll over one edge of the original shape on top of the contrasting fabric and hem it down. For more of a three-dimensional effect, catch each of the four corners together with a few stitches, as shown, instead of hemming.

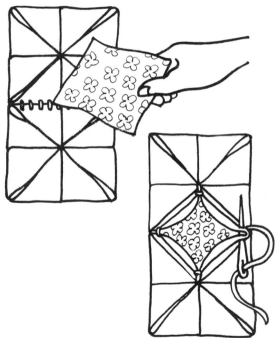

When stitched, pull open, as shown, and flatten out to make a diamond shape. Now, from the center, blindstitch the two open edges together along half the length of the opening as shown. Be sure not to sew through to the back of the fabric.

Turn the square over so that the smooth side is toward you, and one by one, fold the four corners into the center as shown. Stitch all four flaps firmly together in the center, being careful not to catch the back of the fabric.

Make a second folded square following the procedure outlined above; then join the two squares by holding the flat sides together and blindstitching the edges (page 111).

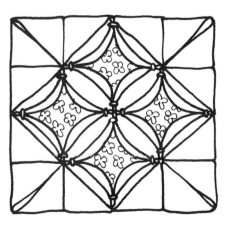

STRIP QUILTS
SEMINOLE INDIAN QUILT

Seminole Indian Quilt, shown in color on page 64, made by Gayle J. Dixon, Idaho.

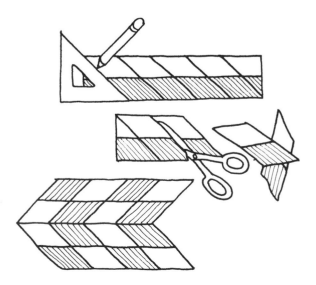

Seminole Indians of southern Florida have developed a variation of the strip quilt technique. Seminole men, women, and children dress in a colorful patchwork that dates from the time when they were driven south from their lands farther north and found their buckskin clothing to be unsuitable for the steamy climate of the Everglades. Every Seminole clan has developed its unique variation of patterns, each with its own special symbolism.

The Seminoles found that strips of bright fabric stitched together, cut across, then turned around and re-joined, could provide a tremendous number of intricate geometric patterns that appear to be extremely complex, yet are really easy to make. If you follow the diagrams, illustrating Band 1 of the Seminole Indian quilt, you will understand the simple principle. Patterns for Bands 2-6 appear on pages 192-193.

Cut or tear on the straight grain four long strips approximately 2" x 80" (or the width of your quilt), plus ¼-inch seam allowances. Cut two strips of one color and two of a contrasting color. Join two different colored strips together along the length. Lay a ruler parallel to the bottom strip and place a plastic triangle (45°) on top. Slide the triangle and mark off a 45° line every 2 inches, as shown. Cut along the penciled lines, reverse the pieces alternately, and rejoin them to make a checkerboard strip. Join two checkerboard strips, matching colors, to form the arrowhead effect shown in the diagram.

138

LISA'S QUILT

Lisa's Quilt, shown in color on page 76, made by Lisa Courtney, Massachusetts.

Lisa Courtney, the prizewinner from Massachusetts, made her own interpretation of Jean Ray Laury's quilt Hills and Valleys, which was designed for velvets and heavy fabrics.

To create your own strip quilt, begin by cutting and joining varying lengths of different colored fabrics to form one strip the width of the finished quilt. The lengths of fabric may vary in width, and the pieces may be joined in any color scheme.

Select a backing material depending on the fabric you used to make the strips. Bold weave cotton or linen is a good backing for velvets; muslin is a suitable backing for strips made of lightweight cotton.

Beginning on the left side of the quilt, machine-stitch the first strip face down onto the backing. (You may find ruled lines on the backing a help for keeping the strips straight.) Lay a length of batting along the wrong side of the strip. Roll the fabric strip over the batting and pin close to the batting along the same line on which you will attach your next pieced strip of colors. Pin the next strip in place, face down, overlapping the first strip, and machine-stitch through all the layers to make a tube. Repeat the procedure until the entire backing is covered.

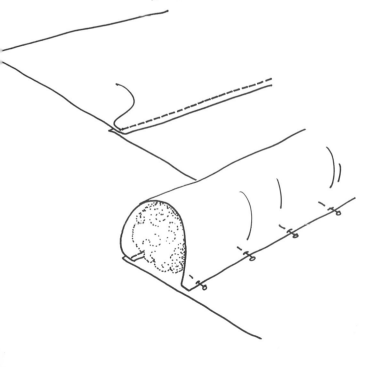

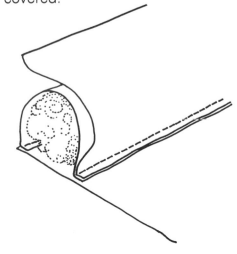

CRAZY QUILTING

Crazy quilts are not pieced and are seldom quilted. They are actually a combination of appliqué and embroidery that originated from a time when scraps too small to be used in any other way were "recycled" by being stitched down to another material. The harlequin effect results from the combination of fabrics of different weights and textures. Silks, velvets, ribbons, printed and embroidered fabrics—all are combined in a collage of colors and textures. Broad bands of embroidery stitches secure the scraps in place, covering the raw edges of the materials (such as velvet, which is too bulky to turn the edges under).

Begin your crazy quilt by mounting a piece of muslin the size of your finished quilt into a square frame (see Frames, page 102). If you plan to construct your quilt by the apartment quilting method, cut the muslin backing into blocks to be joined later.

Since you will be working freehand, you need not outline the design on the muslin. Starting in the center, pin the first piece to the muslin, then the next piece beside it. As you pin, you can either overlap each section by ½ inch or tuck one edge under the other, according to the effect you wish to achieve. Fold under turnbacks with your needle, where they are needed, as you baste each piece in place. Keep all the scrap pieces as flat as possible. If you have a large piece of fabric that would fray without turnbacks, lay it down flat and overlap the edges of the

Welcome My Friends All, crazy quilt, circa 1900. Smithsonian Institution.

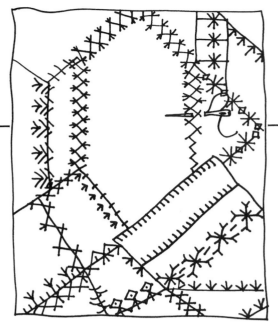

piece with ribbons, which need no turn-backs. Cut some of your velvet pieces with pinking shears, and secure them with the "pinking stitch" shown here and on page 143.

The embroidery stitches are much of the fun of creating a crazy quilt. And it is these decorative stitches worked in contrasting colors of thread that unify and secure all the patches to the quilt top. Experiment with the crazy quilt stitches on the next two pages, adding your own touches.

Crazy quilting may also be done by machine, using a zigzag stitch to secure each patch around the edges. Machine stitching is much easier to do if the quilt is made in apartment size blocks. When joining the blocks into the finished quilt, stitch the blocks together to form strips, then join the strips together, matching the corners carefully (see Quilting, page 111). You may wish

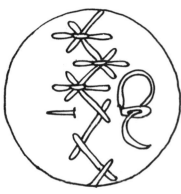

to conceal the joins between the blocks with additional crazy quilt stitches.

To back your crazy quilt, lay the top face down, then lay batting and lining on top. Tuft the layers (see Tufting, page 120), making sure the tufting catches only the muslin, and does not show on the quilt top. Another alternative is simply to line the quilt (without batting), working rows of herringbone stitch across the back, again catching only the muslin backing and not allowing the stitching to penetrate the top of the quilt.

Another Victorian crazy quilt is shown in color on page 7. It is fascinating to compare it and the one opposite with the contemporary Schoolhouse Crazy Quilt on page 54.

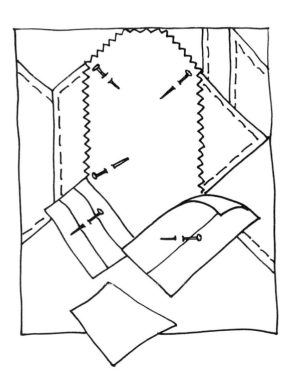

CRAZY QUILT STITCHES

Detail of an album quilt, shown on page 28, made by Pocahontas Virginia Gay, 1900. Smithsonian Institution.

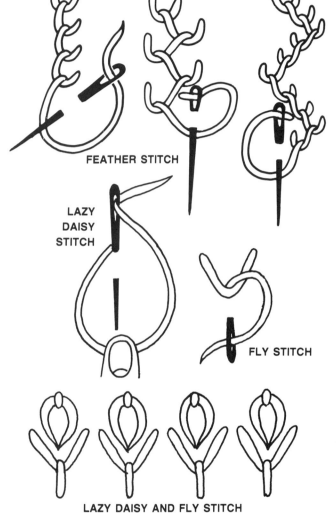

FEATHER STITCH

LAZY DAISY STITCH

FLY STITCH

LAZY DAISY AND FLY STITCH

STAR STITCH

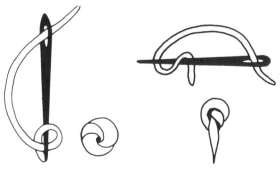

FRENCH KNOT

FRENCH KNOT ON A STALK

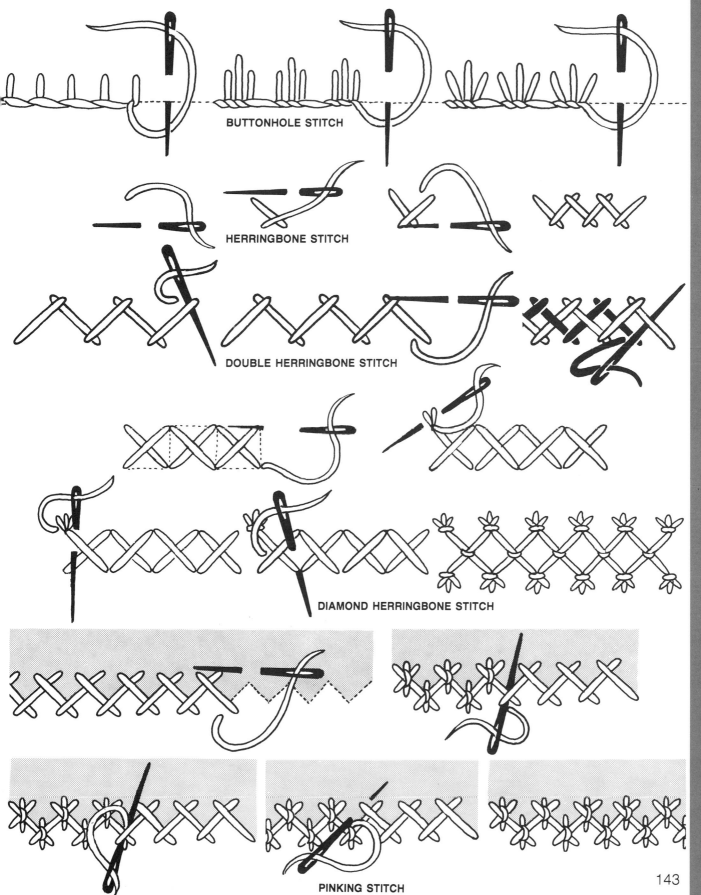

BUTTONHOLE STITCH

HERRINGBONE STITCH

DOUBLE HERRINGBONE STITCH

DIAMOND HERRINGBONE STITCH

PINKING STITCH

EMBROIDERED APPLIQUÉ

Martha Mood's stitching might well be called painting with fabric. She used the texture and color of materials, together with embroidery threads, as an artist might use oil paints. For this technique, it is important to have a wide collection of fabrics to work from so that you can select the colors, textures, and designs that best represent your subject. The relation of one fabric to another must also be considered so that the end result is harmonious.

Begin with a firm backing material that is large enough to cover the entire area of the picture. (Martha Mood used a burlap-linen that was completely covered with appliquéd fabrics when the picture was finished.) Mount the backing in a square frame so that you can see the whole "picture" area at once (see Frames, page 102). As in overlaid appliqué, you build your picture layer by layer, working the underlying shapes first and gradually building towards the uppermost shapes such as the birds, rabbits, and leaves in the foreground. In order to keep the shapes clear-cut and precise, many of the fabrics can be left with raw edges.

To prepare the fabrics for appliqué, use a fine batiste to line the reverse side of a square of the appliqué fabric, bonding the two with fusible interfacing. (Several varieties of fusible interfacings are available; see Suppliers, page 216.) The fabric is held firm with this thin backing, and it can then be cut to shape without fear of fraying. The shapes may be held lightly in place on the background fabric with matching

Detail of America's First Families Number 7, made by Martha Mood.

144

thread or transparent nylon thread.

The embroidery stitches in Martha's design are worked through all the layers of fabric as each area is completed. The stitches can be worked completely freehand, or they can be sketched with an erasable marker so that unwanted lines can easily be removed (see Tools, page 94). A good "naturalistic" stitch for covering raw edges is the slanting satin stitch. Textures such as fur or bark can be suggested with the straight stitch (as on the rabbits shown opposite).

To frame the finished picture with a soft, tapestry effect, fold the backing onto the front to form a narrow binding around the edges (see Finishing, page 158).

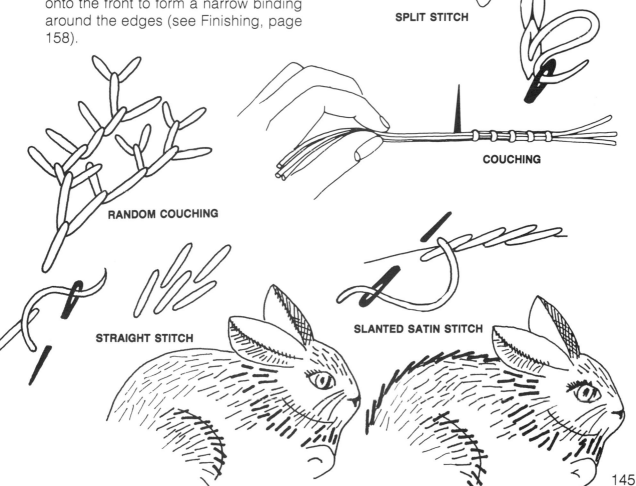

STEM STITCH

SPLIT STITCH

RANDOM COUCHING

COUCHING

STRAIGHT STITCH

SLANTED SATIN STITCH

145

Detail of Maryland quilt, shown on pages 2-3, circa 1850, Otsego County, New York. Smithsonian Institution.

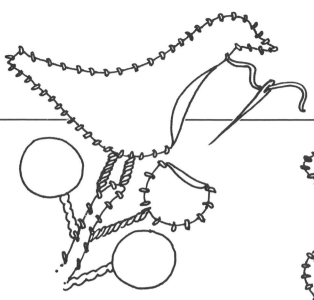

First, outline the design on the background fabric. Next, trace the individual pattern shapes on the fabric to be applied, making sure the grains of both fabrics run in the same direction. (This is shown on the leaf design, page 122.)

Cut out the shapes, allowing ⅜ inch all around for padding and turnbacks. Staystitch around the shape, ¼ inch in from the edge. Clip curves, turn, press, and baste turnbacks to the wrong side of the fabric. Pin and sew shape to the background fabric with small stitches made at right angles to the edges, leaving one section open, as shown. Push cotton in with the points of scissors, stuffing firmly, but not too tightly. Sew the opening closed.

Special textural effects, such as the tufted look shown here, can be achieved by taking small stitches in the center of a padded area.

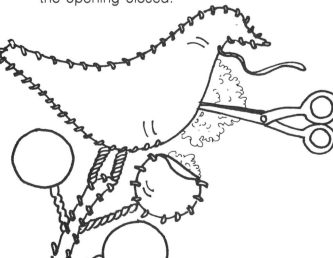

3-D APPLIQUÉ BY MACHINE

Detail of Under the Sea of Eden quilt, shown on pages 42-43, made by Madge Copeland, Arizona.

pages 42-43), the flowers, leaves, people, and fish were all made separately like small flat pillows and then applied to the quilt for an incredible three-dimensional effect.

Since you are using a machine, the petals are easier to make in continuous strips. Fold a long strip of paper accordion fashion, as shown. With curved scissors, cut the petal shape around the upper edge, cutting through all the thicknesses. Fold a long band of fabric in half lengthwise, right sides together. Trace the paper pattern onto the fabric strip; then machine-stitch around the petal shapes, and cut out, as shown. Snip notches in the seam edges, turn inside out, and press to make a strip of smooth, rounded petals. Pad each

In this technique, the shapes are stitched so that they stand away from the background in high relief. In Madge Copeland's marvelous quilt, Undersea Eden (details shown here and on

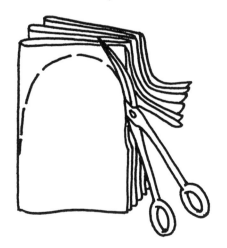

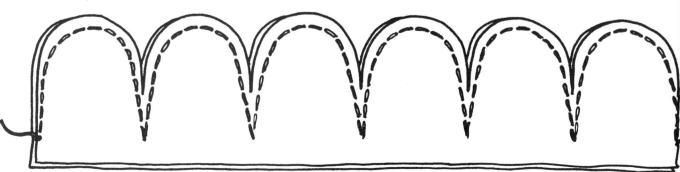

petal lightly, if desired, and pin in position around the center of the flower, taking tucks to create a circle from the straight band, as shown.

Cut a circle of fabric for the overlapping flower center large enough to allow for turnbacks and padding and to cover the raw edges of the petals. Snip the turnbacks and press to form a smooth circle. Baste the center in position, slip in a few cotton balls as shown, and machine-stitch around the circle with an open zigzag stitch.

For this kind of three-dimensional appliqué, it helps to visualize your finished shapes by first cutting roughs from graph paper, pellon, or crinoline, and then taping the pieces together. When the size and form are correct, untape the design and use the pieces as a pattern for cutting out your fabric shapes. Because of the size and scope of her quilt, most of Madge's stitching was done by machine. Flowers and leaves are fastened to the background fabric by the centers and long central veins; the tree trunk was stitched in contoured lines to resemble bark. Details where a raised, but not three-dimensional, effect was needed (such as the fish and human figures) were stitched to the background fabric by hand, catching the appliqué shape with small stitches from the reverse side.

3-D APPLIQUÉ BY HAND

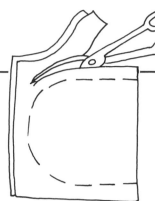

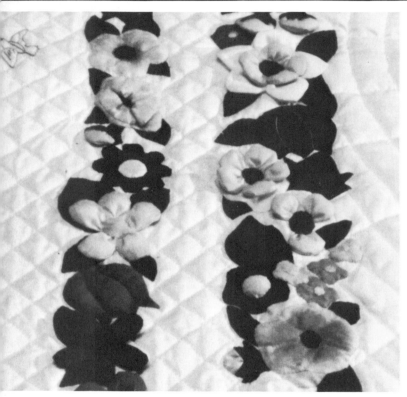

Detail of Camellia Cameo quilt, shown on page 77, made by Annie Sellers Davis, Alabama.

The Camellia Cameo quilt by prize-winner Annie Sellers Davis shows how three-dimensional flowers, stitched by hand, can blend perfectly with traditional quilting to make a contemporary, yet classic, quilt.

The effect of high and low relief is produced by first stitching some of the underlying leaves and flowers in padded appliqué (page 146). The free-standing flowers are then made by stitching the petals down separately.

To make a petal, cut out the desired shape from a doubled piece of fabric, leaving a wide opening at the mouth that will later be gathered for a puffy effect. Stitch around the outer edge of the petal, leaving the mouth open. Trim and snip the turnbacks. Before turning the petal inside out, open and flatten the seam allowances by pressing them back with your thumb and forefinger. When the petal is turned inside out, the seam will then be smooth and flat. Lightly stuff the petal shape, if desired, and run a gathering thread across the mouth. Hold a group of petals in place with a round center of padded appliqué.

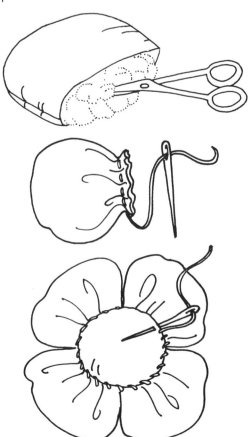

150

For variety, create a flower with a base ring of petals worked in padded appliqué and three-dimensional petals on top, as shown in the photograph.

Another method of making three dimensional flowers by hand eliminates the need for drawing the petal shapes first. To make the petals, cut a circle of fabric, fold it in half, then double it over and run a gathering thread along the curved edge, as shown. You can connect five or more petals with this gath-

under the last flap of a cardboard box. Hold each triangle in place with pins and run a gathering thread around the outside edges. Draw it up to form a circle and stitch in place in the center of the ring of petals. To pad, open the center of the circle and push the stuffing in.

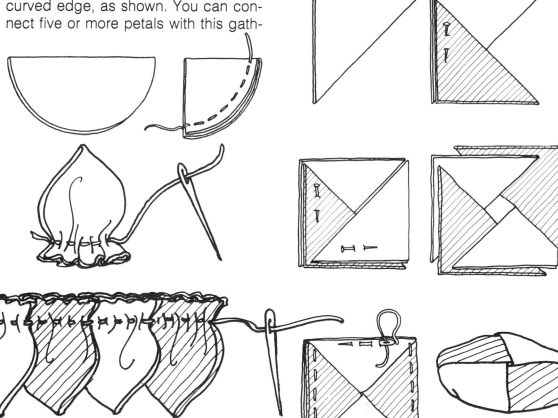

ering thread, and then draw it up into a circle to make a ring of petals.

For the center, cut four squares, fold in half diagonally, and fit the four triangles together as shown, overlapping each and tucking the fourth triangle under the first, just as you would fold

RUCHING

Detail of Maryland quilt, shown on pages 2-3, circa 1850, Otsego County, New York. Smithsonian Institution.

This unusual technique may have originated with the Queen Anne ribbon work of eighteenth century England, but it was extremely popular in Maryland in nineteenth century America. The beautiful example shown here and on pages 2-3 was worked with narrow strips of material, cut on the bias, folded, gathered, and then applied to the background fabric. Today, bias binding is excellent for this purpose.

Stitch the binding by hand or by machine in a "V" line as shown in the drawing. Gather the binding up and stitch it to the background fabric (raw edges down) with small, invisible stitches taken with matching thread.

You will get a different effect if you double the bias binding or if you vary the amount of "waviness" in the gathering line. Try combining ruching with padded appliqué, embroidery, and quilting (as in the example from the Smithsonian) for an unusual and attractive effect. Starting in the center, you can spiral the gathered fabric around in widening circles, as shown; you can use it as an outline; or try weaving rows of it under and over to form a basket.

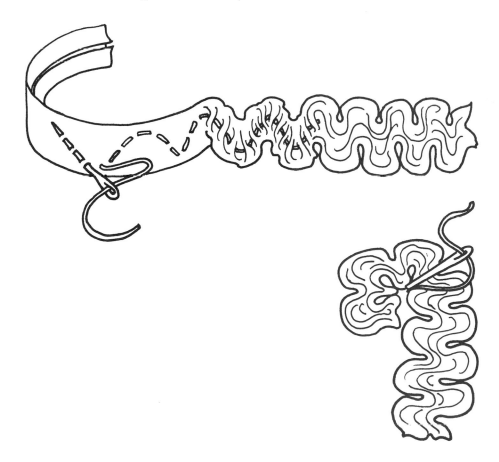

The Winner's Circle and Noah's Ark quilts shown on pages 52-53 appear at first glance to be appliquéd, but actually the designs are painted on the cloth with fiber-reactive dyes or fabric paints.

An increasing number of products are available today for treating fabric with paints, dyes, and crayons. (See Suppliers, page 216.) Perhaps the simplest to use are wax crayons, which become permanent after ironing your cloth. First, fill in the areas to be colored

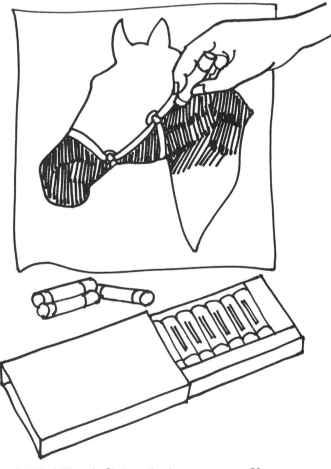

Detail of Winner's Circle quilt, shown on pages 52-53, made by Yukon Norman, Utah.

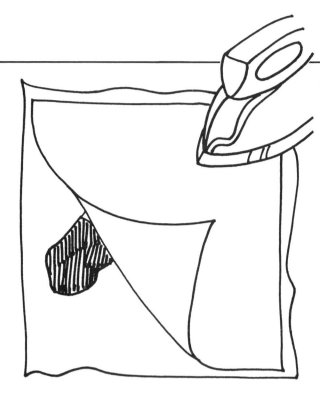

on your fabric with the crayons, as shown. Cover the ironing board with a protective cloth, lay the fabric with the colored design on top, cover with aluminum foil, and iron to "set" the colors. A slight oil ring may appear around the design, but this can easily be washed out with soap and warm water.

Embroidery paint is available commercially in a wide variety of colors. It is permanent, washable, quick-drying, and the colors can be mixed and blended. The paint is available in tubes with a ball-point tip, which is excellent for thin line work, or the top can be removed for use with a brush. When working with a brush, be careful that the paint does not "run." The paint should be of such a consistency that it flows onto the fabric smoothly without bleeding. Do not load the brush too heavily with paint, especially when working close to an outline. To use embroidery paint, stretch out your fabric either with masking tape or in a hoop. Keep blotting paper under the fabric to absorb excess paint.

Fiber-reactive dyes produce clear, vivid, transparent colors and can be applied in a dyebath, or painted directly on the fabric. They are quite easily used. The dye is sold in powdered form, which is mixed with urea, a thickening agent, washing soda, and water. The urea and thickener are available from most suppliers of the dye; the washing soda can be purchased from the grocery store.

Although these dyes are no more dangerous than ordinary household dyes, they are a chemical substance and should be used carefully. The dye powder is milled so finely that a dust mask should be used while handling the powder. Care should also be taken in storing and clean-up to avoid distributing the powder into the air. Food, coffee cups, cigarettes, etc. should be kept out of the work area to prevent any contamination, and gloves should be worn to prevent contact with the skin.

PHOTOGRAPHY & YOUR QUILT

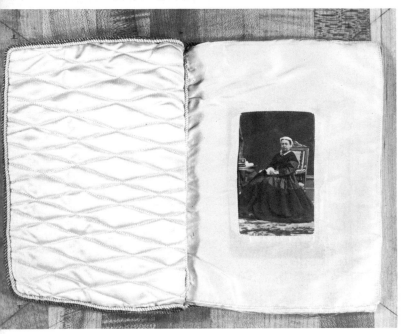

Photograph of Queen Victoria printed on silk. From Historic Photographs on Cloth *by Mary Stieglitz. International Museum of Photography. Eastman House, Rochester.*

Transferring images to fabric can add another dimension to your quilting. Photography, discovered almost simultaneously by Daguerre in France and Talbot in England, was popularly recognized in 1839. Fascinatingly enough, what may have been the first photograph ever printed on cloth was made in the following year, when John Mercer invented mercerized cotton.

Karee Skarsten's Niagara Falls quilt on page 41 is a beautiful example of blueprinting on fabric. Called the "ferro-prussiate" process, it was developed by Sir John Herschel in 1830 in England when he discovered that iron was sensitive to light. Simply prepare your cloth with an iron-based emulsion, and when it is exposed to the light, it will turn Prussian blue. By this means you can transfer to your fabric such things as leaves, lace, cutout paper shapes, or photographs.

FINDING YOUR PHOTOGRAM

The images you transfer are called "photograms." As well as negative or positive photos, you can transfer a high-contrast photograph that has a graphic, almost silhouette effect. Called a "line conversion" print, this process is ideal for the purpose because it has almost the look of a woodcut, rather than a realistic photo. Photocopying services can provide various sizes of line conversion prints done on acetate (transparent film).

PREPARING THE FABRIC

The best fabric for this process is 100% cotton. This should be stretched tightly and smoothly on artists' stretcher strips available from the art supply store. Assemble the strips to form a square, and with a heavy-duty stapler, secure the taut fabric on all four sides. Wash the stretched fabric in the bathtub to remove all sizing; then leave it standing in the tub to dry.

PREPARING FOR PRINTING

Work in a well-ventilated, darkened room. *The Cyanotype blueprint emulsion (recipe below) is poisonous,* so be sure to wear rubber gloves and do not allow the emulsion to contact anything but the fabric. Place the fabric, stretcher strips up, on a protected surface (plastic sheeting on top of newspaper), and apply the emulsion evenly, working first in one direction and then in the other. Now turn the stretcher over

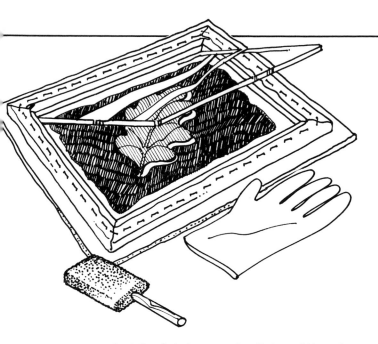

so that the fabric can dry flat and the air can circulate underneath.

THE PRINTING PROCESS

Working in the darkened room or a shady spot out of doors, lay your dry fabric, *stretcher strips up,* on a firm surface (such as felt-covered foam core board). Lay your photogram on top (dull side down if you are using a photo-negative). To press it firmly down and make good contact, place a heavy (¼-inch thick) sheet of glass flat on top.

To expose indoors, use a sunlamp three feet away held by a clamp. Outdoors, move the whole thing into the bright sunlight. Exposure time can vary from two minutes to one hour, so it is a good idea to test-print some small swatches first. The color will turn from chartreuse to bright green to dark green to blue and finally to blue grey, at which time you will know it is "ready." If overexposed, you will lose detail and the color will be deep blue; if underexposed, the image will not hold.

DEVELOPING THE IMAGE

Rinse the stretched fabric under the shower or hose for two to three minutes until the image is clear. To intensify the image and clear the surrounding fabric, steep it for thirty seconds in water to which a "glug" of 3% hydrogen peroxide has been added. Afterwards, always wash with mild soap, and never use bleach. You can also experiment with other emulsions and formulas that will give you different colors. Recent discoveries have made it possible to print with a range of clear colors (see Suppliers, page 216).

Another method of transferring images to cloth is by photocopying. Susan Murphy's Gum Wrapper quilt on page 44 was made by transferring the image of gum wrappers to satin, using a Xerox copying machine. This can be done relatively inexpensively by the Trans Seal 300J method, which prints on extremely thin film that is then permanently transferred to the fabric by means of heat. Photocopiers can perform the entire process for you.

CYANOTYPE BLUEPRINT EMULSION
Precaution: *Poisonous.* Wear rubber gloves. Clean the bowl between each mixing. Use no metal.
A. ½ ounce potassium ferricyanide
   ½ cup distilled water
B. 1 ounce ferric citrate
   ½ cup distilled water
Mix A and B separately and store in separate brown bottles. Allow four days for aging. When ready for use, pour equal parts of both into one bowl. Mix only what you need because the mixture loses effectiveness after approximately twelve hours.

FINISHING

One of the most popular ways of finishing the edge of a quilt is to bring the lining over the top and blindstitch it around the edges for a narrow binding. The lining should always be cut larger than the quilt top and the batting in case you decide to use this easy finish.

Bias binding is another excellent way of finishing the edges of a quilt. Since the edges receive the most wear, it is a good idea to double the bias fabric. Stitch it to the top of the quilt, right sides facing; then turn it over and hemstitch it to the lining, easing it around the corners as shown.

On a quilt with a wide border that looks as though it were added afterwards, the border may actually have been stitched and quilted at the same time as the rest of the quilt. The top and the lining were brought together at the edges, trimmed evenly, turned under, and blindstitched (see page 111) so that there is no discernable edge.

Should you prefer an unquilted border that is slightly wider than a bias binding, it can be attached in the same manner. In this case, corners may be treated in one of three ways: (1) Simply

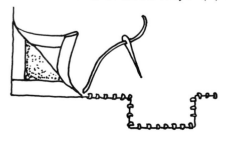

double over the hem on one edge of the quilt, then double the other edge on top of it, as shown, hemming right through. Just be sure that both horizon-

tals or both verticals overlap in the same manner.

(2) Trim a little of the turnbacks away after folding and hemming as in (1); then appliqué a square of fabric over the corner, as shown.

(3) Many people are unsure of themselves when it comes to mitering, but a mitered corner is really very easy to do if you first make a paper pattern the same size as your hem. On a square of paper, fold over a double hem on both sides of one corner. Crease the paper sharply. Open the paper and you will see four squares at the corner. Cut diagonally through the two center squares, as shown. Fold back to the point of the last remaining square, as shown, then turn down the double hems and you have a mitered corner.

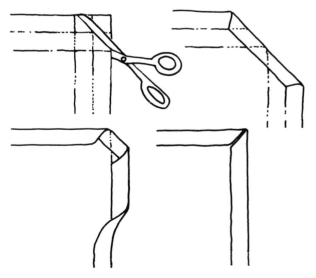

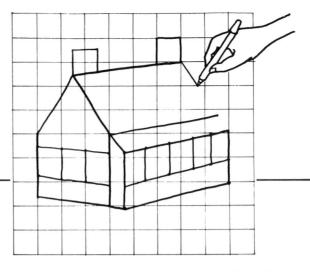

HOW TO USE THE PATTERNS

All the techniques needed to work with any of the following quilt patterns are included in this book. Simply use the special index tabs along the right-hand pages to help you quickly locate the particular technique called for.

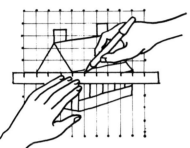

Wherever possible, pattern pieces are given actual size. When patterns must be enlarged, simply connect the dots across the design; you will then have a grid of squares over your pattern. Take a piece of tracing paper slightly larger than the size you want your finished design to be, and lay it on

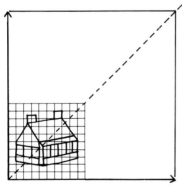

top of this book, fitting the design into the lower left corner of the tracing paper. Rule a line to project diagonally (from corner to corner) on the tracing paper, as shown, until you reach the size you want. Extend and connect corner lines, making sure that all corners are true right angles. Cut the new square or

rectangle out of tracing paper, fold it into the same number of squares as you have marked in the small drawing, rule colored lines over the fold lines, and copy your pattern in the larger scale, square by square.

Actual-size patterns do not include seam allowances or turnbacks. (See page 130). To prepare the shapes for piecing, trace them on acetate, card-board, or sandpaper, using a perma-nent marker, and cut them out to use as templates. Draw around the pattern pieces with a pencil or a marker on the wrong side of the fabric. To reverse (or "flop") patterns, simply turn the tem-plates over when marking the fabric. The marked lines will be your seam lines. Be sure to cut ¼ inch beyond these lines to allow for seams and turn-backs.

Enlarging can also be done by pho-tostating. Companies listed under "blueprinting" in your phone book can prove invaluable when you want to en-large a complex design. Simply give one measurement to the photography service and the rest will follow propor-tionately.

To transfer a complex design to the fabric, trace it first onto organdie, tulle (fine netting), or sheer muslin, using a fine marker or pencil. Tape your fabric to a firm surface, then tape the organ-die with the design on top, and trace again using a permanent marker. Test to see if the ink is penetrating the fab-ric—a fine, yet clear, line should result.

RAY OF LIGHT

JINNY BEYER
VIRGINIA
Color, pages 46-47
Quilt measures 80¼" x 90"

Technique: Hand piecing.

Quilting: Hand quilting.

(1) Center medallion: outline rays of "Mariner's Compass," radiating lines of quilting out to the points of the sawtooth border of the central diamond.

(2) Sawtooth pattern: quilt just inside the seam line, making a small triangle inside each sawtooth shape.

(3) Four corners completing central square (detail on page 112): fill each corner with two feather patterns (pages 108-109). In the open space between each pair of feathers, outline three small leaves. As a background, work bunched quilting or "strippling"—stitching in close rows to flatten the fabric and silhouette the puffed feathers and leaves.

(4) Diamond borders: quilt parallel, V-shaped rows inside each triangle. On the larger diamond borders, this contour quilting shows more clearly. In each triangle (between the small medallions, for instance), four parallel rows are worked. Repeat the same technique on each of the other borders. The small "Mariner's Compass" diamonds in the outer border are quilted just like the large center medallion, continuing the rays out to the edges of the square.

Assembly: You will find this quilt much more interesting to make if you follow Jinny Beyer's idea to "build as you go," adapting the design to your own requirements instead of following every detail precisely as it is shown.

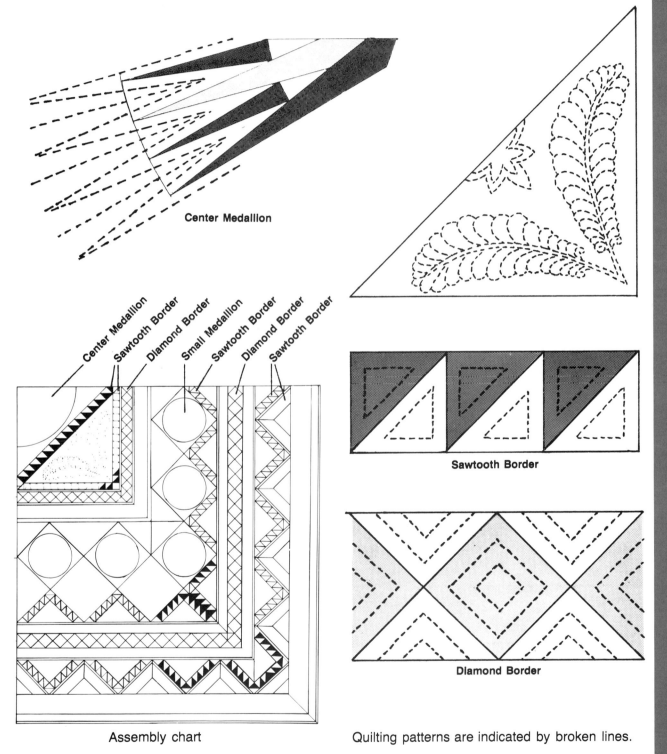

Center Medallion

Center Medallion   Sawtooth Border   Diamond Border   Small Medallion   Sawtooth Border   Diamond Border   Sawtooth Border

Sawtooth Border

Diamond Border

Assembly chart

Quilting patterns are indicated by broken lines.

161

Center medallion

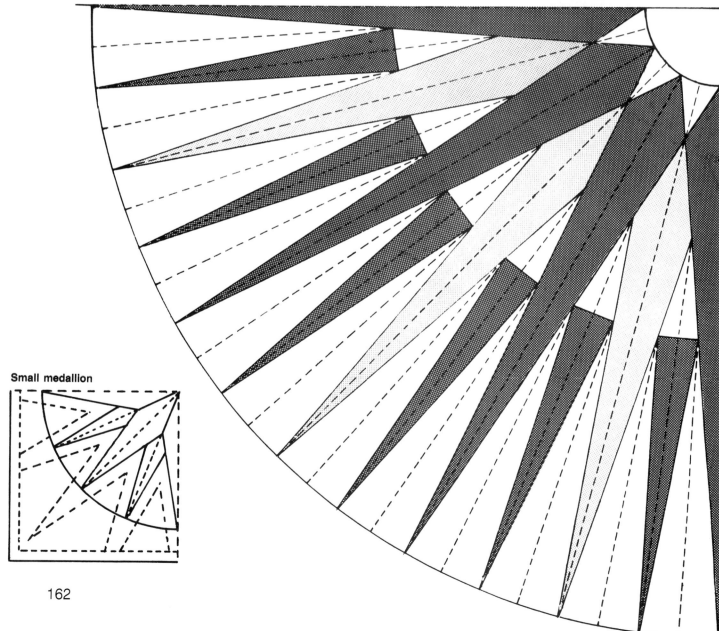

Small medallion

162

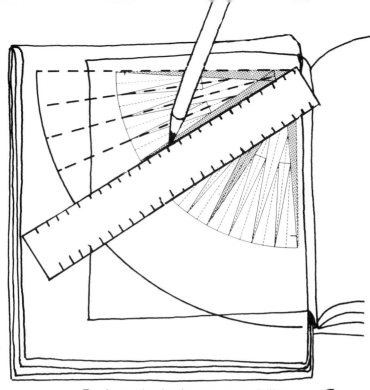

Tracing and enlarging center medallion

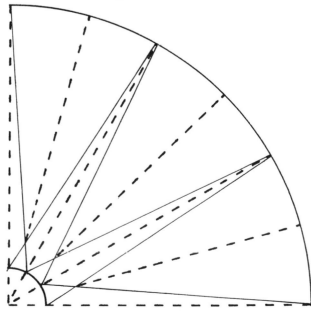

Alternative: Constructing center medallion with 30° triangle.

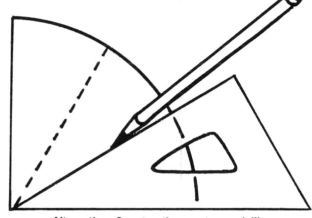

Drafting Center Medallion: (1) Place a square of tracing paper diamond-fashion in the center of your bed. When you have determined the size you want, fold the square in fourths to establish the center with crease lines. Open the paper up, and with a compass, draw a circle to fit within the square, leaving 2 inches of clearance between the circle and the edge of the square.

(2) Place one quarter of your pattern over the quarter center medallion on page 162. Using a ruler, trace the *broken* lines that radiate from the center circle, extending the lines to fit your circle, as shown. Whatever the size of *your* medallion, the broken lines radiating from the center circle will always be in the same position.

(3) Move on and trace the remaining three quarters of the center medallion, accurately marking the radiating lines.

(4) Tape the tracing to a firm surface and draw the inner circle with a compass. Now connect the points of the medallion, starting with the darkest first. (Notice that there are four—north, south, west, and east—and two in between. Altogether there are twelve dark points running right to the center circle.) Each dark point extends from the five broken lines on the inner circle to a single point at the outer circle, as shown in the diagram opposite.

Alternatively, you can construct the center medallion by working with a 30° triangle. Draw one quarter of the design and divide it, as shown. Then continue, forming the compass points explained above. The smaller medallions are constructed in the same manner.

(5) Rule the next ring of points as described in step 4, finally working to the third ring of points on the outside.

163

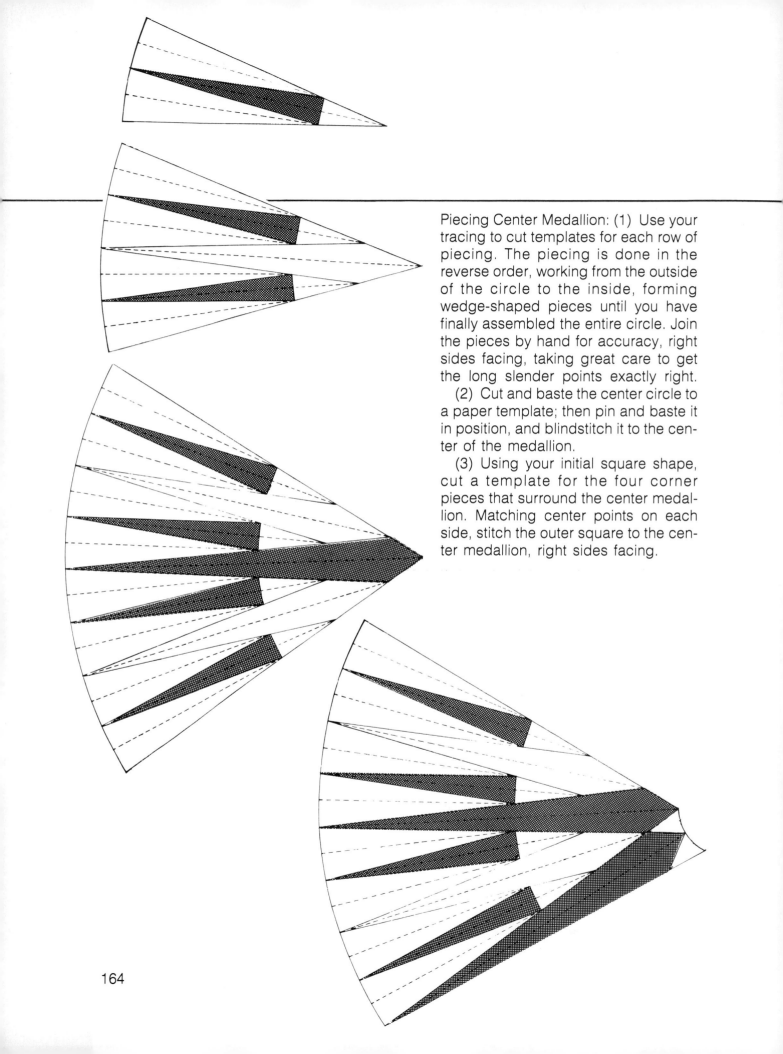

Piecing Center Medallion: (1) Use your tracing to cut templates for each row of piecing. The piecing is done in the reverse order, working from the outside of the circle to the inside, forming wedge-shaped pieces until you have finally assembled the entire circle. Join the pieces by hand for accuracy, right sides facing, taking great care to get the long slender points exactly right.

(2) Cut and baste the center circle to a paper template; then pin and baste it in position, and blindstitch it to the center of the medallion.

(3) Using your initial square shape, cut a template for the four corner pieces that surround the center medallion. Matching center points on each side, stitch the outer square to the center medallion, right sides facing.

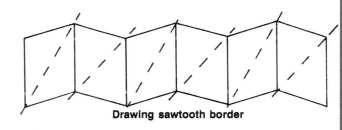

Drawing sawtooth border

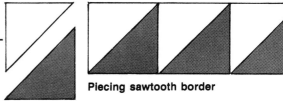

Piecing sawtooth border

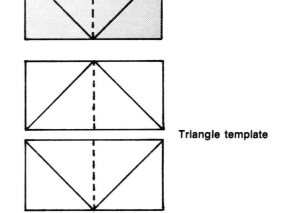

Diamond template

Triangle template

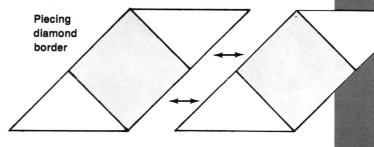

Piecing diamond border

Drafting Sawtooth Border: (1) Cut a strip of paper the exact length of one side of your central square and about 6 inches wide. Fold it in half and in half again, and continue folding until you have divided it into small segments. Measure the size of one segment and cut the width of the strip to that size so that you form exact squares.

(2) Rule a line diagonally through the center of each square to form two triangles. These will be your templates for the sawtooth border.

(3) Piece the border, alternating dark and light triangles.

Drafting Diamond Border: (1) Construct templates for this border by folding paper in the same way as for the sawtooth border. Remember, it must always be based on the square to avoid trouble at the corners. In other words, the width of each segment must equal the width of the border. The fewer the number of segments, the wider the border; the more segments, the narrower the border. To make the diamond, fold each square in half and in half again, and connect the crease lines, corner to corner. Each triangle equals one-half a diamond.

(2) Cut paper templates and follow the technique described for hand piecing hexagons on page 132, joining the pieces as in the diagram. You can also piece the diamond border by hand, right sides facing.

For the smaller medallions in the diamonds and for all the other borders, follow exactly the same procedures described for the center of the quilt, using the assembly chart on page 161 as a guide. The quilt is rectangular because an extra row of dark diamonds was added to the top and bottom borders. By simply eliminating them, you can make the quilt a perfect square. Feel free to construct different borders by this method, interspersing them with bands of plain fabric to make your own version of Ray of Light.

Finishing: Pieced strip border or double bias binding in matching fabric.

DRAW ME

**LINAE FREI
NEW YORK**
Color, pages 48-49
Finished block measures 20″ x 20″

Technique: Embroidery, straight stitch and stem stitch (page 145).Sashing pieced by machine. Blocks joined by machine.

Quilting: Button tufting (page 120).

Assembly: (1) Outline animal shapes on graph paper, using only straight lines, exactly like a "connect the numbers" children's puzzle. To get you started, four animal patterns are given on the next pages; find other simple shapes in coloring books or draw your own designs.

(2) Mark a grid on each block of background fabric by folding and pressing; then machine-stitch along the lines in self-color thread in each direction as a guide for your stitching. With embroidery wool, outline the animal shapes with long straight stitches, following the graph and adding touches of embroidery and appliqué (spots for giraffe, tusks for elephant).

(3) Piece the sashing by machine in gaily colored squares of fabric. Join vertical strips of sashing to the animal blocks to make horizontal rows, then join the rows with horizontal sashing taken the entire width of the quilt.

(4) Using a color that unifies the entire quilt, stemstitch along the seam line where the horizontal sashing meets the blocks. Cover the seams where the vertical sashing meets the blocks with a narrow binding.

(5) Baste batting, lining, and quilt top together and button-tuft with pearl blouse buttons sewn down at each corner of the machine-stitched grid.

Finishing: Edge the quilt with narrow binding.

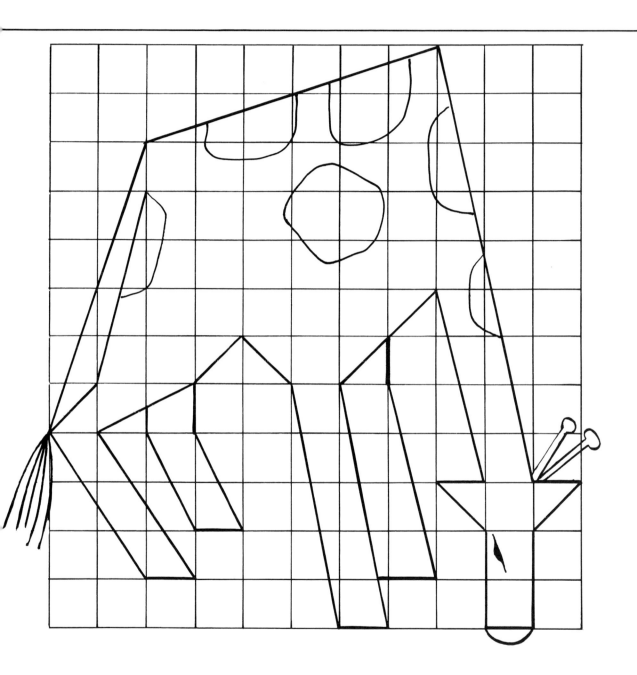

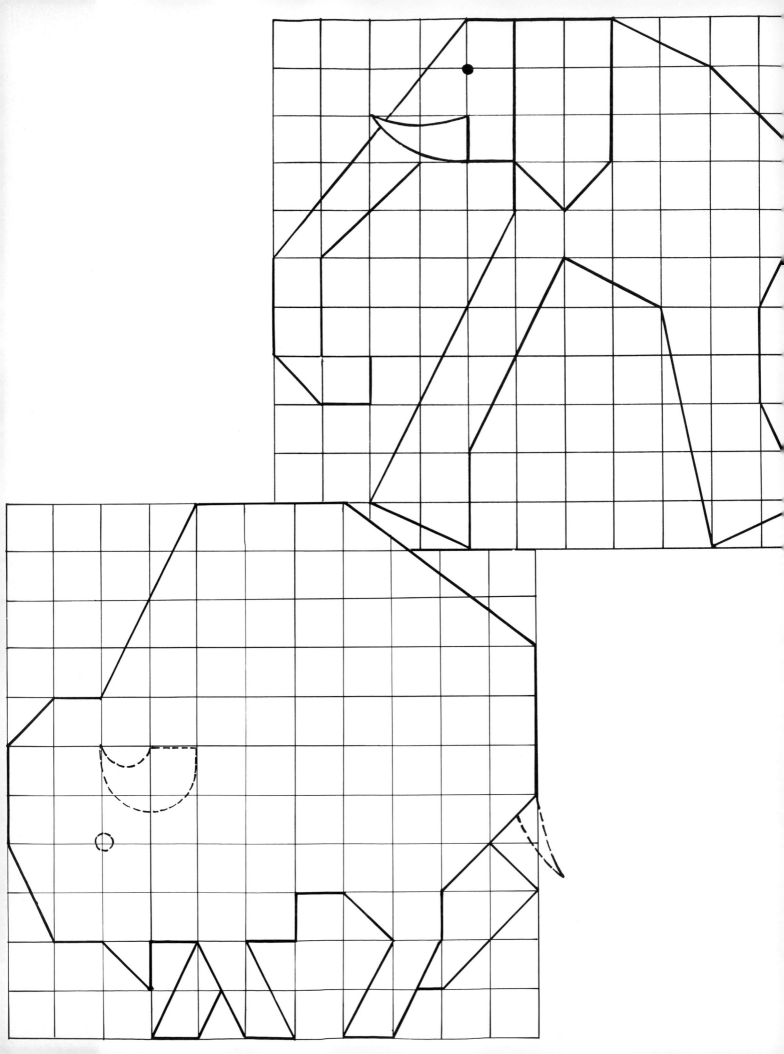

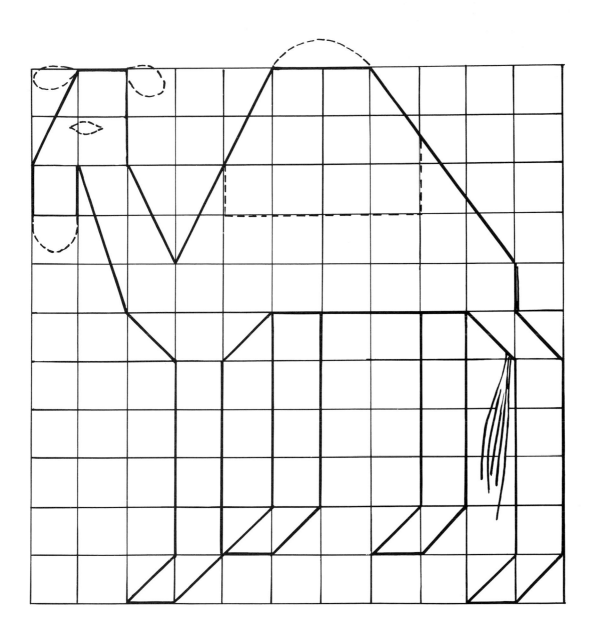

WANDA DAWSON
NEBRASKA
Color, pages 50-51
Quilt measures 92″ x 100″

Technique: Hand piecing.

Quilting: Outline quilting.

Assembly: Since hexagons call for extreme accuracy in fitting, units of this size are best joined by hand, following the instructions on page 132. Trace the template on the opposite page.

Finishing: Binding made from a 5-inch-wide bias piece. Fold the doubled strip lengthwise to make a 1¼-inch finished binding on either side of the quilt.

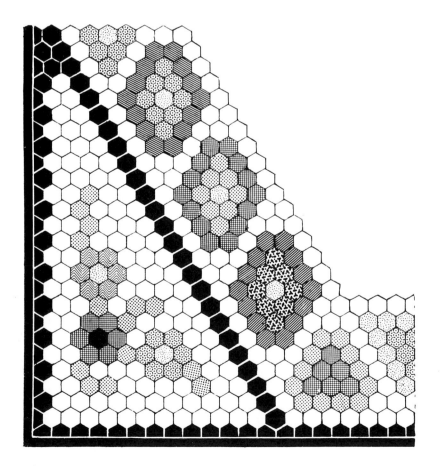

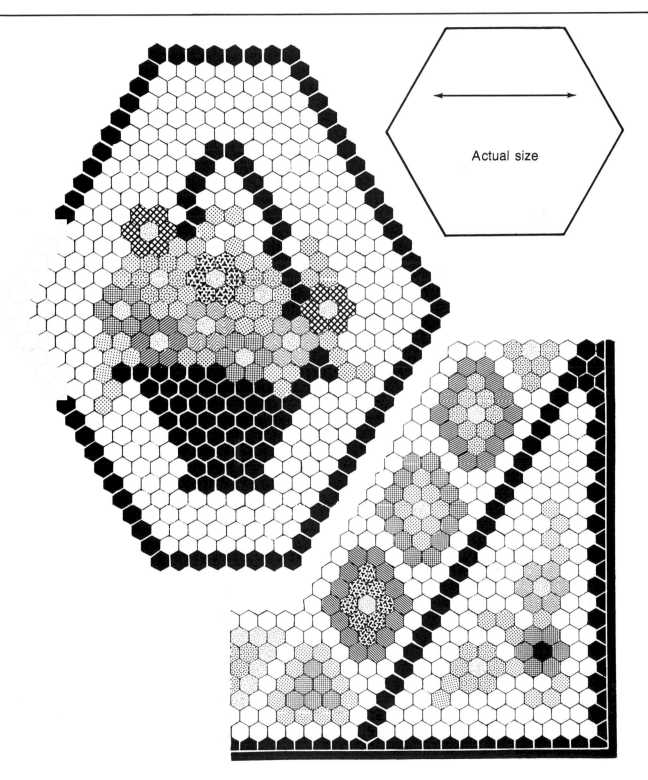

Actual size

**YUKON NORMAN
UTAH**
Color, pages 52-53
Quilt measures 83¾" x 94½"

Technique: Painting fabric, appliqué, and machine or hand piecing.

Quilting: Tufting and machine or hand quilting.

Assembly: This quilt looks best if the pieced border of squares lies at the edge of your mattress, so establish the size of your quilt accordingly.

(1) Begin with the central horse's head. You can either appliqué it in brown fabric and only paint the eye, halter, and blaze, or you can paint the entire head and the oval around the head, quilting around all the outlines afterwards to make it appear like appliqué. Since the horse's head is such a simple silhouette, you can cut a template of the pattern and use that for your appliqué or your painting.

(2) Enlarge the pattern for the central head on page 174, following the procedure explained on page 159. Draw the horse's head to the required size in the center of a sheet of paper large enough to contain the central ovals as well.

(3) Fold the paper in fourths with the sketch outwards. Draw one-fourth of the oval pattern, following its position on the large grid exactly as it appears on the smaller one. Cut through all four thicknesses along this outer line. Open the paper and you have a perfect oval.

(4) To make a template for the patchwork pieces around the oval, overlay one quarter section of the enlarged oval with tracing paper. Draw a line parallel to and 5¾ inches beyond the outside of the oval as shown in the diagram opposite. Now fold the tracing paper in half diagonally, and in half again, and then in half once more. Open the paper and you will have eight sections delineated by the crease lines, as shown by broken lines in the diagram opposite. Label the pieces sequentially before you cut out the templates, because each one will be slightly different; then cut along the broken lines. Number the reverse side of the templates as well, because you must "flop" (turn over) the patterns for the two opposite quarters so that they fit around the oval.

(5) Using these templates, cut and piece the patchwork oval either by hand or by machine. Appliqué it in position around the inner, solid-colored oval.

(6) Piece the square border using the pattern opposite, and join it to the

center square.

(7) The outer borders measure 11 inches wide with 11-inch square blocks in the corners. When corners and outer borders are complete, draw a grid with tailor's chalk or a marker, and tuft the central square of the quilt. Leave loose ends on the back of the quilt.

Finishing: Use double bias binding or bring lining over the front of the quilt to give the effect of a piping.

Actual size
Cut 192
2 rows of 20, top and bottom.
2 rows of 28, both sides.

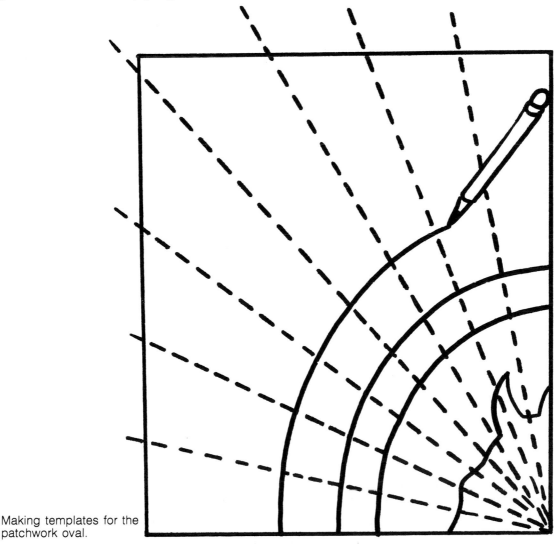

Making templates for the patchwork oval.

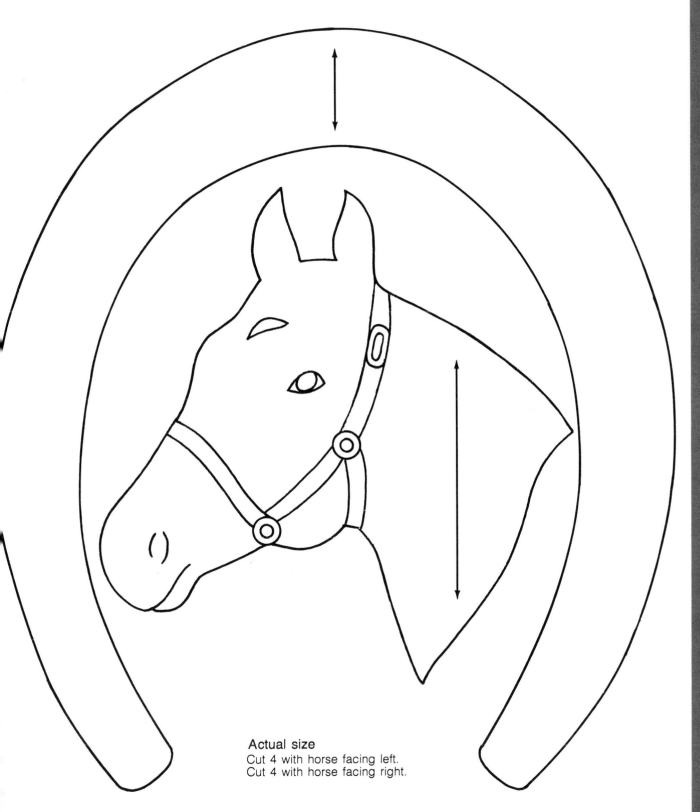

Actual size
Cut 4 with horse facing left.
Cut 4 with horse facing right.

Assembly chart

176

Quilting pattern; actual size

Arrange as you wish, 6
across the top and bottom,
7 down the sides.

MARA FRANCIS
CONNECTICUT
Color, page 54
Quilt measures 80″ x 100″

Technique: Combination of crazy quilting (page 140) and overlaid appliqué (page 124), by hand.

Quilting: None

Assembly: (1) Enlarge on paper the design opposite and transfer it to muslin (page 159) to use as a background, labeling each section both on the paper pattern and on the muslin.

(2) Then, as in overlaid appliqué, cut apart your paper pattern, creating pieces like a jigsaw puzzle which you can use as guides for cutting the fabric. When cutting your shapes out of fabric, allow *at least* ¼-inch for turnbacks. If the material is too bulky for turnbacks, yet is not liable to fray, you can always trim away any excess after the piece is in place, but if a speck of muslin shows through, you can't add!

(3) Baste each piece down, as discussed in Crazy Quilting. Secure the edges with feather stitching, herringbone, and stem stitch, etc. (pages 142-143 and 145) exactly as they appear in the color photograph.

Alternatively, create your own "village" starting with houses (patterns on the following pages) and grouping them in a pleasing arrangement on the muslin. Roads, trees, and lakes can then be cut and pinned down to cover the muslin completely—exactly like a crazy quilt—adding embroidery stitches to secure as well as decorate the entire design.

Finishing: If desired, interline the quilt with a thin blanket to give it body, and then back it with a suitable material. Bring the lining over the front of the quilt to create a binding, mitering the corners (page 158).

Assembly chart

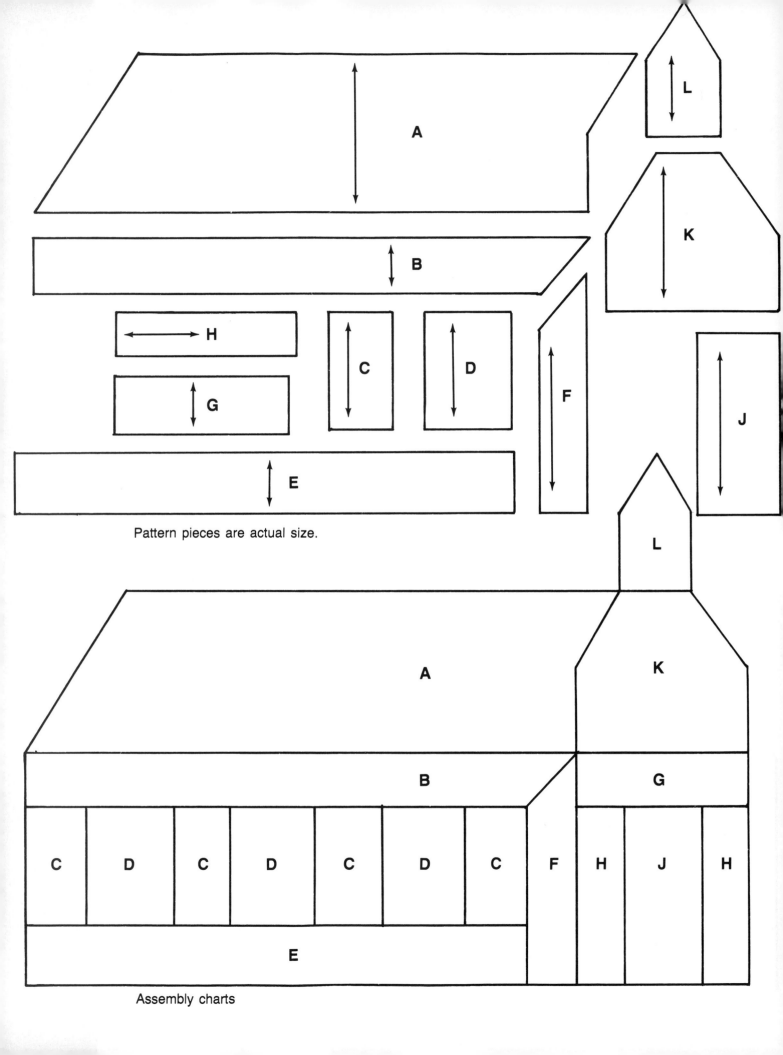

Pattern pieces are actual size.

Assembly charts

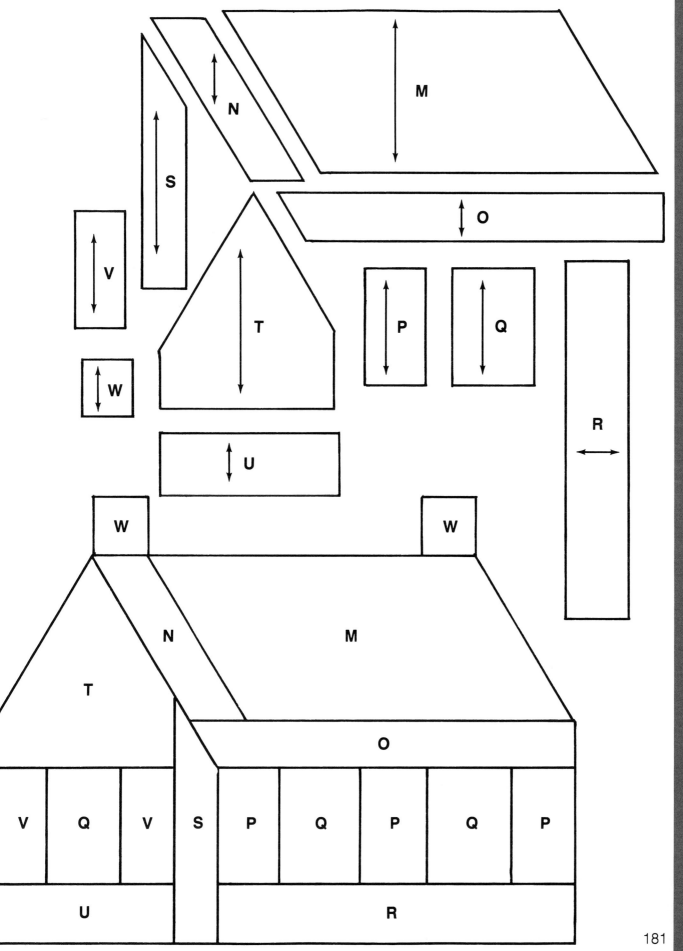

**NANCY KOUNTZ
PENNSYLVANIA**
Color, page 59
Quilt measures 95¾" x 94"

Technique: Machine or hand piecing based on squares. To make the Q-U-I-L-T quilt, follow exactly the pattern given; color variations are shown by shading on the graph. Or, create your own design with whatever word or letters you would like by simply "building" the letters out of squares.

Quilting: Contour quilting by hand or by machine, following the outline of the squares.

Assembly: (1) Work out your entire design on graph paper to decide how many squares of each color are needed for each letter, and how the words will fit together.

(2) Join squares in vertical strips, by hand or by machine, following your graph. Then join the strips to repeat the design across the width of your quilt.

Finishing: Blindstitch the edge of the quilt top to the lining.

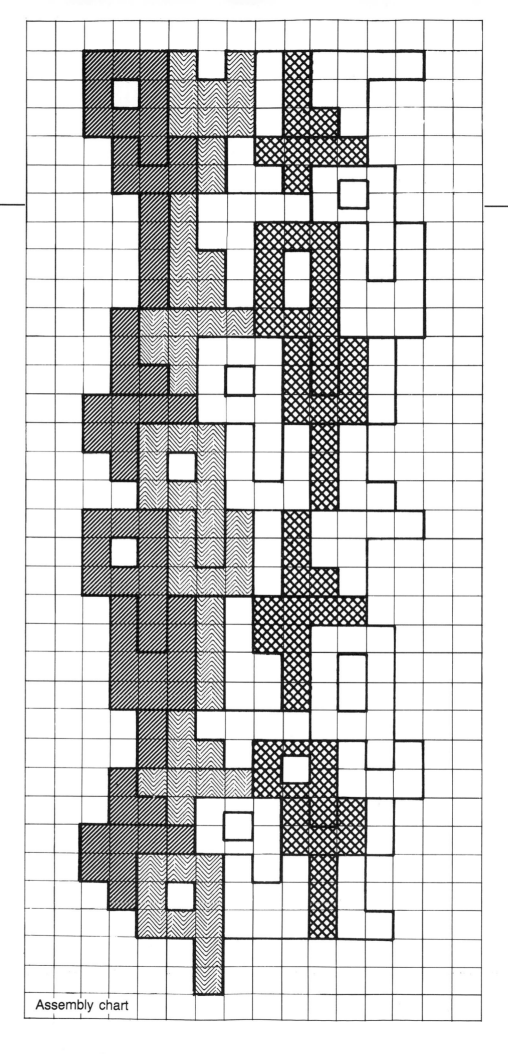
Assembly chart

BEACH SOLITUDE

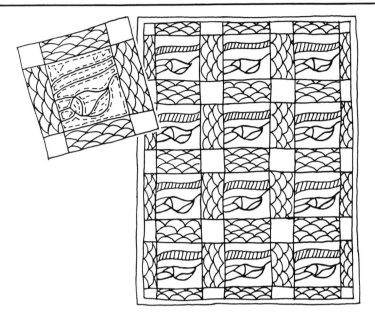

ANN HUMPHRIES
FLORIDA
Color, page 61
Finished block measures 11″ x 11″

Technique: Hand piecing.

Quilting: Outline quilting on either side of the seam lines and contour quilting on the sea shell. Sashing squares are quilted in the shell pattern, indicated by broken lines below.

Assembly: For absolute accuracy on the curved lines of the shell, it is best to piece these shapes by hand, using the method illustrated on page 132. Sky and sea may be joined as shown on page 124.

Finishing: Completed blocks should be joined with vertical sashing strips to make a horizontal row of three. When these are joined you will have four rows to be joined with long strips of pieced horizontal sashing. The border sashing is exactly half the width of the center sashing, and the whole quilt is finished with a broad binding.

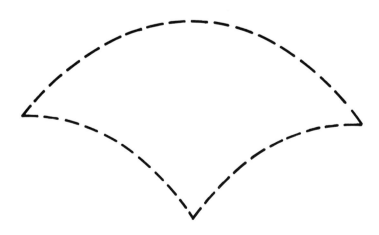

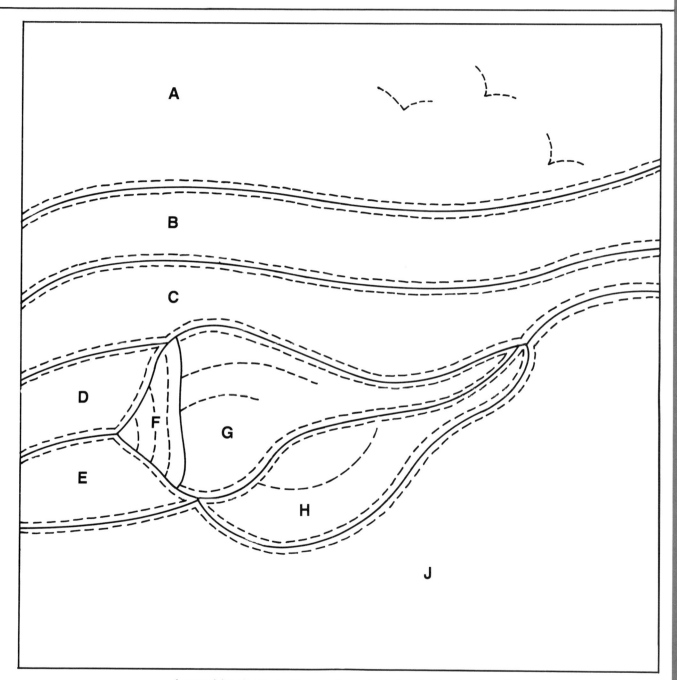

Assembly chart; quilting pattern is indicated by broken lines.

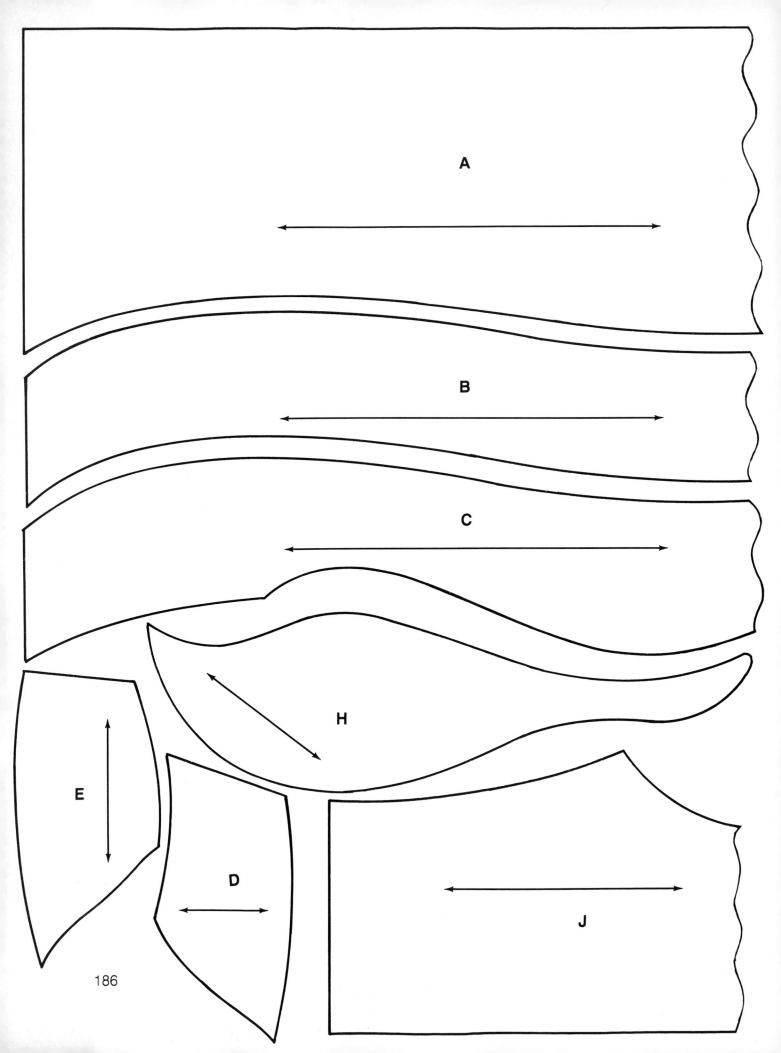

A

B

C

H

E

D

J

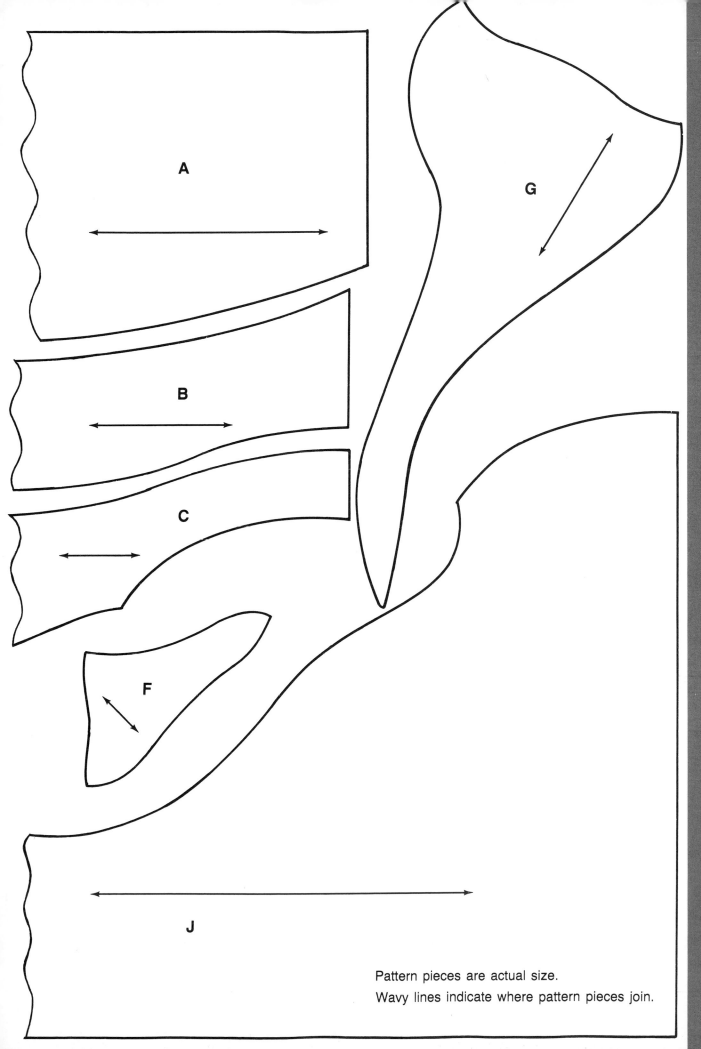

A

B

C

F

G

J

Pattern pieces are actual size.

Wavy lines indicate where pattern pieces join.

SUNSET SEA

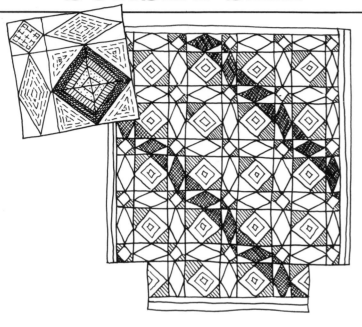

MARGARET BOESCH
RHODE ISLAND
Color, pages 62-63
Finished block measures 18″ x 18″

Technique: Machine piecing. Because of the complex color scheme, it is a good idea to make a color chart on graph paper so that you will know exactly how many pieces of each color are needed for your pattern. In the assembly chart opposite, you will notice triangles labelled D and D₁. After you have cut the fabric with the D template, you must flop it to cut the fabric for the D₁ pieces.

Quilting: Contour quilting, following the shapes of the pieces in parallel lines, by hand.

Assembly: To plan the color scheme, follow the Block Assembly Chart on the opposite page.

(1) Start by piecing the small square in the lower right-hand corner of the diagram. Begin with small triangle J, and work out, joining H, G, F, and finally large triangle E, to form a square. Make three other squares in the same manner; then join all four of the squares to form large square 1.

(2) Next, piece rectangle 2a in the top right of the diagram. Join it to the top of the large square assembled in step 1.

(3) Piece rectangle 2b and square 3 and join together.

(4) Join the two parts together to form one complete block, shown opposite.

Finishing: Piece the border with a narrow center strip between two wide ones. Sunset Sea was made for a four-poster bed with cutouts for the posts, but the pattern can simply be continued to make a rectangle. Finish outer edge with a 1½-inch bias binding.

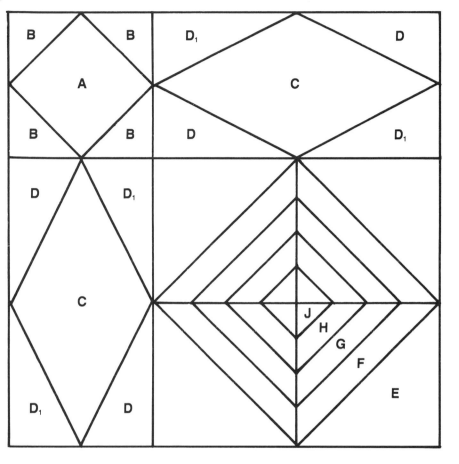

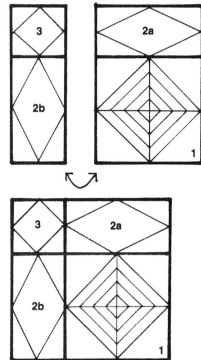

Joining the Block: Assemble block 1; then join it to 2a. Join 2b to 3. Finally, join these two pieces together to form one complete block.

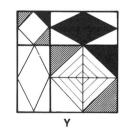

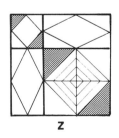

X   Y   Z

Block Assembly Chart: If you compare the blocks above with the drawing on the opposite page, you will notice that the darkest band of blocks (X) runs diagonally through the quilt. Dark blue is represented by black in the diagram and the medium blue is represented by grey. The other colors in the original quilt—reds and cream—remain constant; only the dark and medium blue shades change with each block (patterns are on the next page).

Z	Y	X	Z	Y
X	Z	Y	X	Z
Y	X	Z	Y	X
Z	Y	X	Z	Y
	X	Z	Y	X

189

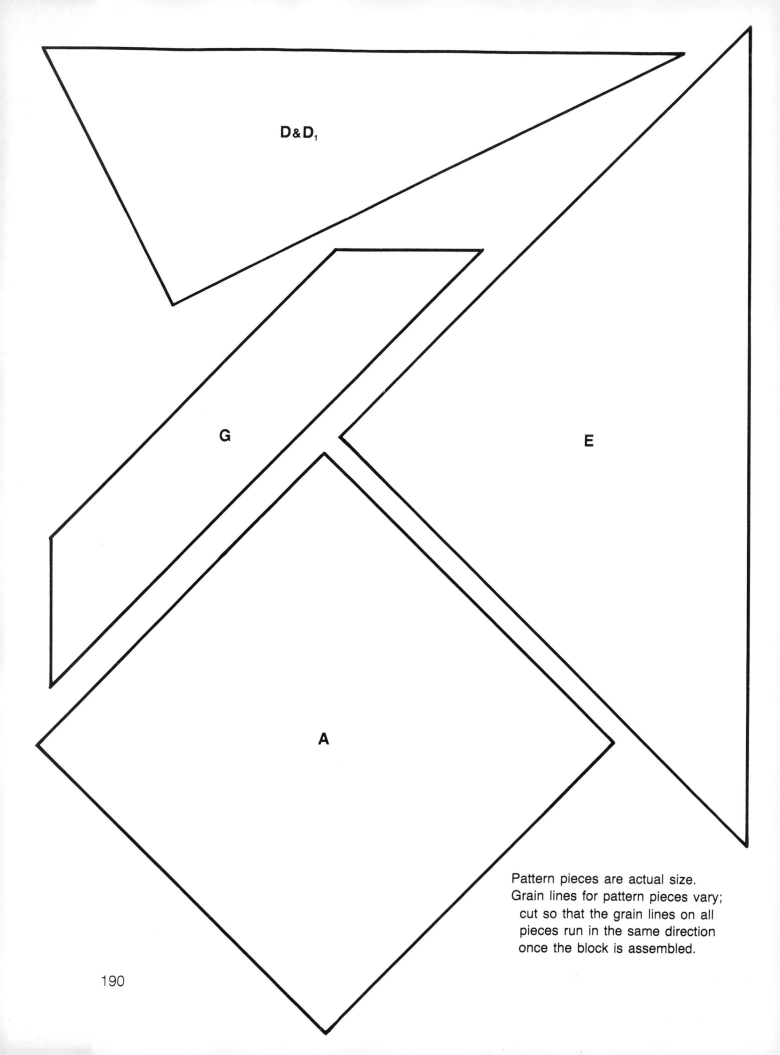

D&D₁

G

E

A

Pattern pieces are actual size.
Grain lines for pattern pieces vary;
cut so that the grain lines on all
pieces run in the same direction
once the block is assembled.

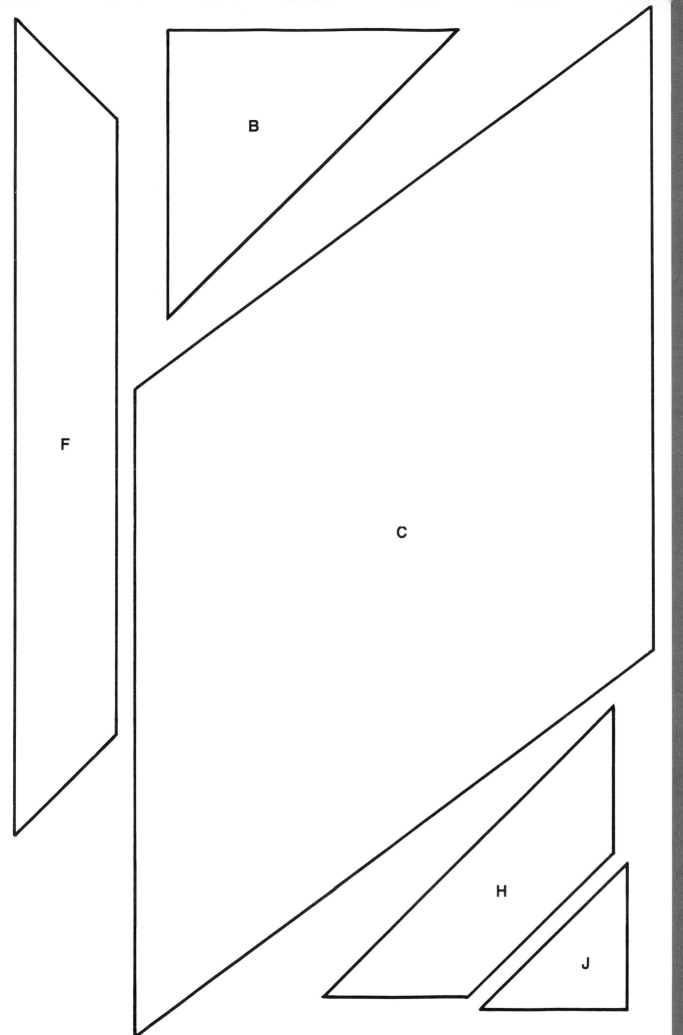

B

F

C

H

J

SEMINOLE INDIAN QUILT

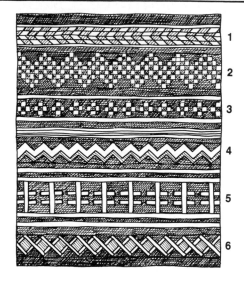

GAYLE J. DIXON
IDAHO
Color, page 64
Quilt measures 80″ x 78″

Technique: Seminole piecing with strip technique (page 138).

Quilting: Hand or machine quilting following the seam lines or cutting across the center of a square, as shown by the broken lines in the diagrams of Band 2, step 2 and Band 3.

Assembly: Follow the charts on the opposite page and the basic assembly instructions on page 138. Start with the top border and work down, band by band, following the band numbers on this page and the diagrams opposite.

Figure the length of each band according to the width you wish your finished quilt to be. Experiment with different widths of fabric; you will be amazed at the number of patterns you can create by simply varying colors and widths. Diagrams for Band 1 are shown on page 138.

Straight strips of color can be stitched between the bands if desired; for instance, strips of contrasting colors are stitched between Bands 3 and 4. Straight borders also frame Bands 3 and 5.

Finishing: Edge the quilt with narrow double binding or blindstitch the backing and the quilt top together.

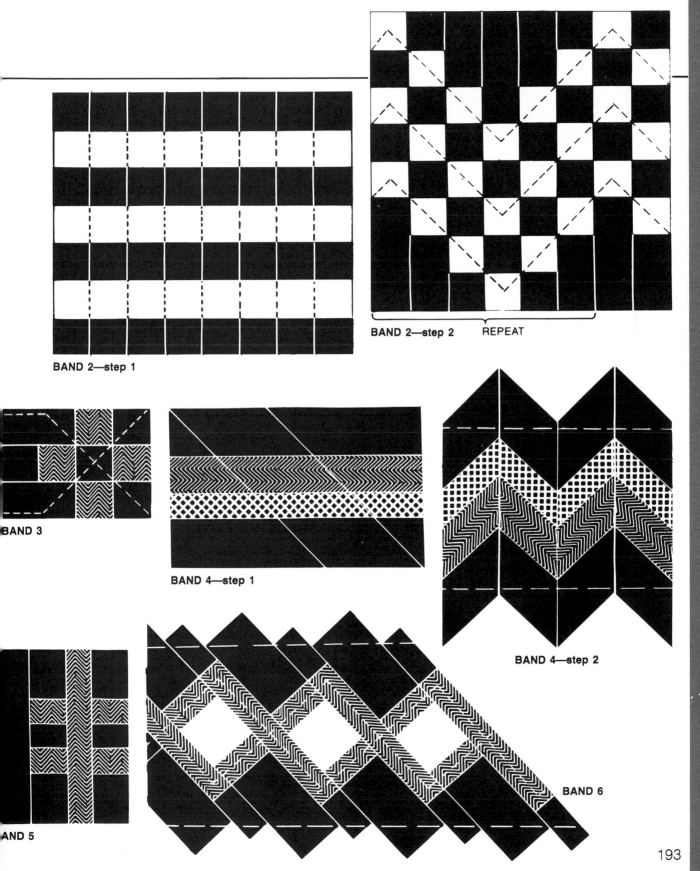

BAND 2—step 1

BAND 2—step 2   REPEAT

BAND 3

BAND 4—step 1

BAND 4—step 2

BAND 5

BAND 6

AUTUMN LEAVES

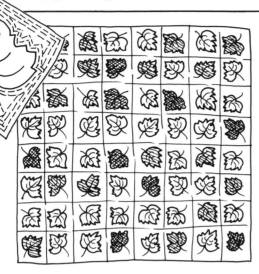

KAREN HAGEN
WEST VIRGINIA
Color, page 68
Finished block measures 8″ x 8″

Technique: Hand appliqué (page 122). Blocks joined by machine.

Quilting: Three rows of close contour quilting surrounding the leaf shapes, blending into wider spacing of straight-line quilting inside each background block.

Assembly: (1) Appliqué the leaves to the background square of fabric. Grain lines are not marked on the pattern because they will vary according to how you position each leaf on the background block. Delineate the veins and stems by working stem stitch (page 145) in four strands of six-strand cotton floss.

(2) Join the blocks in strips, then join the strips together, or join them after the quilting is complete if you are using the apartment quilting technique (page 111).

Finishing: Bring the lining over the front of the quilt for a narrow binding.

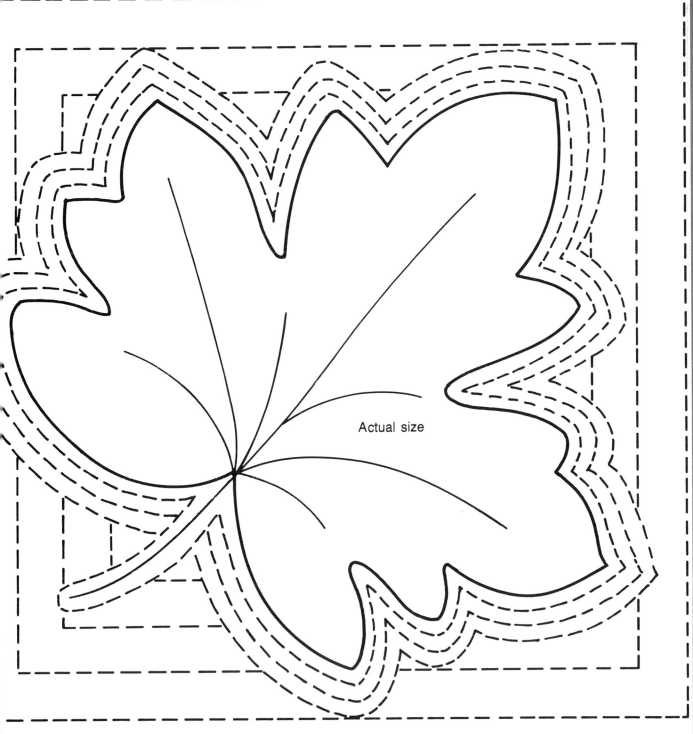

Actual size

Quilting pattern is indicated by broken lines.

BUTTERFLIES

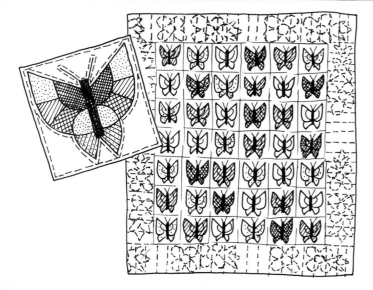

**MRS. HUGH VAUGHN
SOUTH DAKOTA**
Color, page 69
Block measures 9¾" x 10"

Technique: Machine piecing and hand appliqué.

Quilting: Hand quilting, outlining block and butterfly. The border can be quilted with simple leaf and flower shapes and a background of parallel lines.

Assembly: One-half of the butterfly pattern is given. For the second half, simply flop pattern pieces A-F before cutting the fabric.

(1) To assemble one wing, join pieces A, B, C, and D in a strip by hand or by machine. Next, join piece E to the lower part of the strip and join piece F to the upper part to complete one wing.

(2) Flop the templates to cut the pieces for the other wing, and assemble it in the same manner. Be careful not to stretch curved edges.

(3) When both wings are completed, prepare them for appliqué (page 122) by staystitching, pressing, and basting the turnbacks down all around, except for the edges that will lie underneath body piece G. With contrasting thread, baste the center line in both directions on your background fabric block. Pin both wings in position on either side of the line; then appliqué the body in the center, letting it overlap the wings as shown.

(4) With four strands of a six-strand black cotton floss, outline the wings and stitch the antennae with stem stitch (page 145).

Finishing: Attach a wide border in a contrasting color and quilt as explained above.

Pattern pieces are actual size.

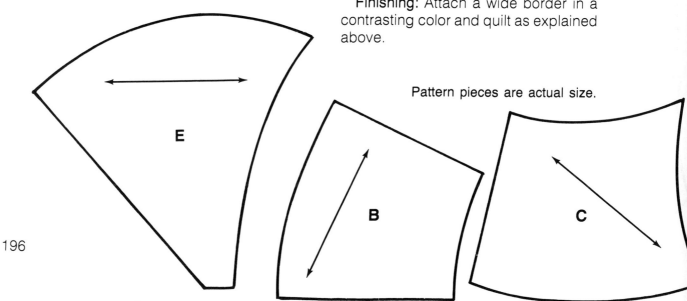

196

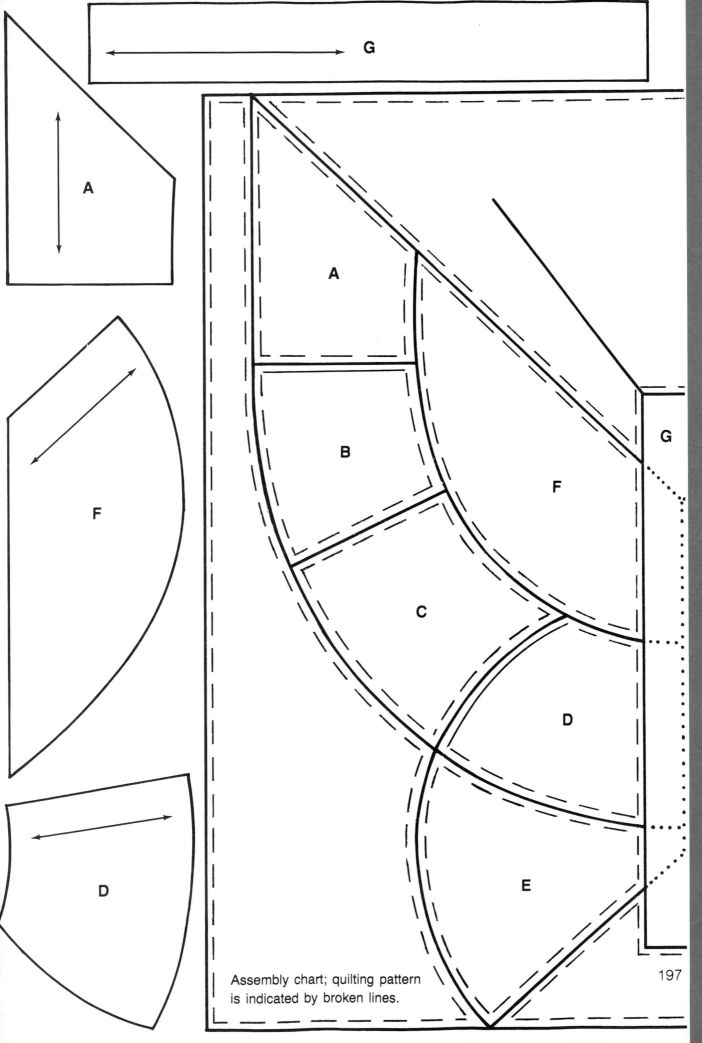

G

A

F

D

G

A

B

F

C

D

E

G

Assembly chart; quilting pattern
is indicated by broken lines.

197

MY GARDEN QUILT

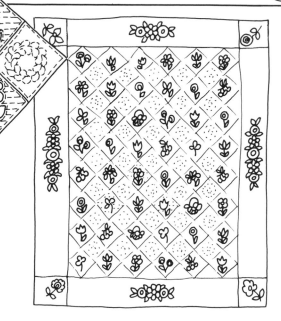

WALLA DOLESKI
MICHIGAN
Color, page 72
Finished block measures 7½" x 7½"

Technique: Overlaid and layered appliqué by hand (pages 124-125). Blocks joined by machine.

Quilting: Outline quilting around flowers. Straight-line quilting in a grid pattern as a background in each block and in the border (page 200). Circular feather design quilted in each of the plain white blocks between the appliquéd blocks (page 106).

Assembly: The patterns for the fruits and flowers of My Garden Quilt were made by drawing around spools of thread and glasses of different sizes on colored paper. The circles were then cut out and glued on top of one another in a pleasing color scheme. Stems and leaves were added in different shapes for variety. Four patterns from the quilt are shown actual size on the following pages.

(1) Appliqué each flower onto a block diagonally, and set the blocks together in a checkerboard of diamonds. With this simple formula you can design your own flower garden, filling each diamond shape to make a colorful contrast with the alternating white diamond. Before assembling your quilt, appliqué all the squares, then lay them on the bed and arrange and rearrange the order until you find a balanced, pleasing design.

(2) Set the diamonds together in diagonal strips; then join the strips, alternating appliquéd blocks with plain ones. A white triangle is needed at the end of each row to even out the saw-toothed edge (see diagram).

(3) Attach four strips for the border, each with a central grouping of flowers. Set a square with an appliquéd flower design into each of the four corners.

Finishing: Bring the lining over the front of the quilt for a narrow binding.

D

F

E

B

C

A

Pattern pieces
are actual size.

Grain lines vary on unmarked pieces; cut so that the grain lines run parallel to background fabric.

B

B

C

B

C

C

A

C

C

B

D

F

E

Assembly chart

Assembly chart; quilting pattern is indicated by broken lines.

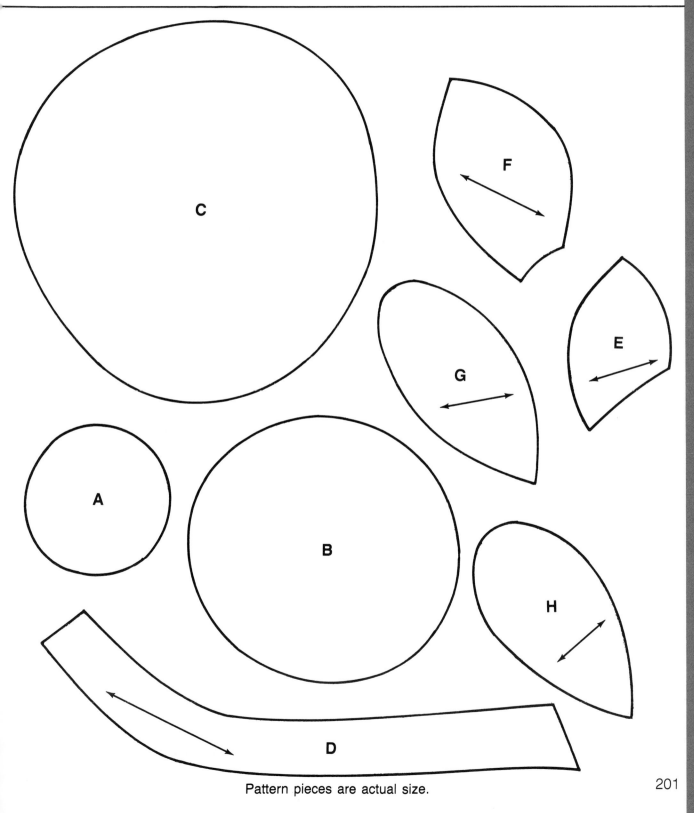

Pattern pieces are actual size.

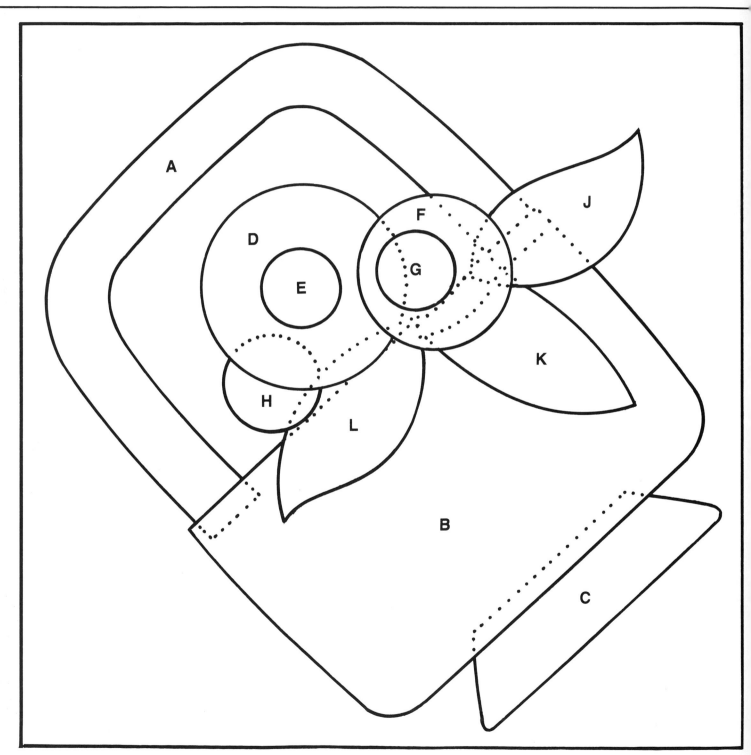

Assembly chart

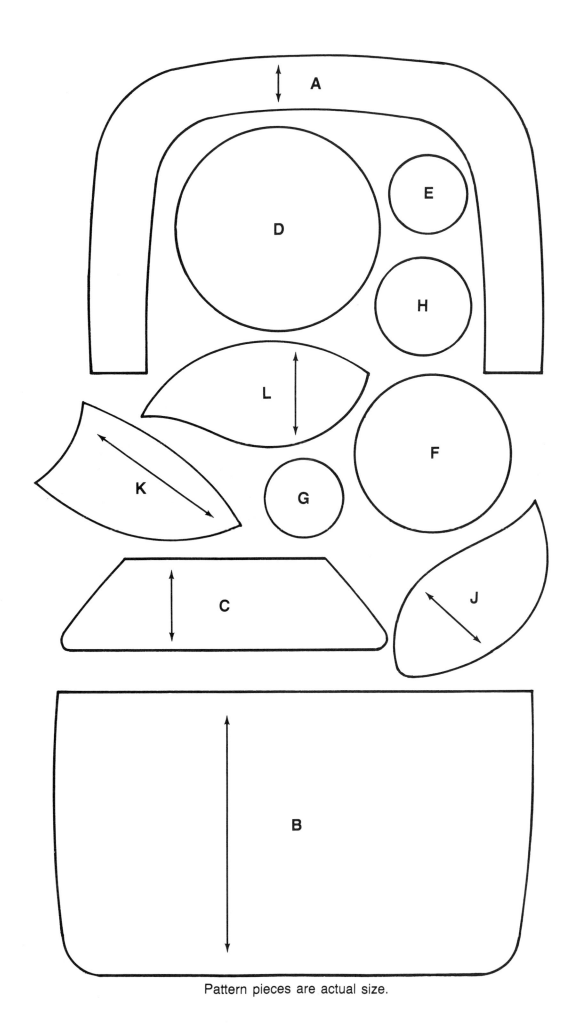

Pattern pieces are actual size.

TRAPUNTO II

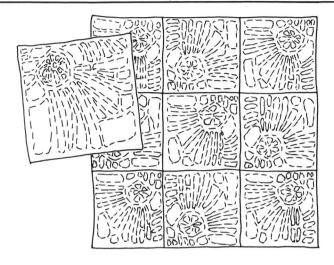

**RHEBA WRIGHT
ARIZONA**
Color, pages 72-73
Finished block measures 30" x 32"

Technique: Machine trapunto (page 114), using double-knit fabric.

Quilting: Outline quilting by hand, one line on the outside of the machine line.

Assembly: (1) Enlarge and trace the design onto muslin and baste to the reverse side of your fabric. Working on the reverse side (muslin side up), machine-stitch around all the outlines in self-color thread. Stuff large areas. Join blocks together.

(2) Baste batting and lining to reverse side.

(3) Quilt by hand on the right side, working one row of quilting stitches around the outside of the machine-stitched line. Or, quilt each of the blocks individually and join the blocks when all are completed, using the apartment quilting technique (page 111).

Finishing: Binding made from a wide bias strip that is stuffed with batting and then hemstitched to the backing.

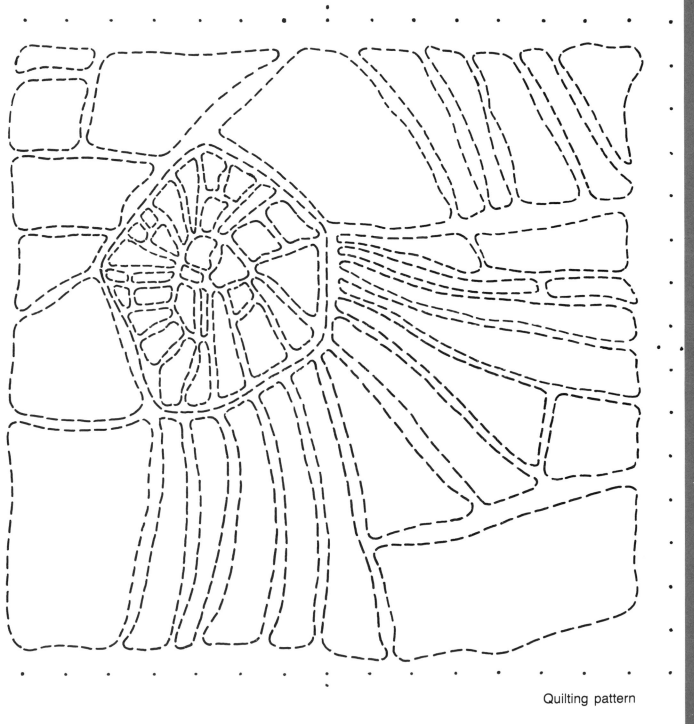

Quilting pattern

LEDA

JANNY BURGHARDT
WASHINGTON, D.C.
Color, page 74
Quilt measures 80″ x 81″

Technique: Center motif, hand appliqué. Inside borders, machine appliqué and piecing.

Quilting: Outline quilting surrounding shapes, and contour quilting in hair and free flowing border design.

Assembly: (1) Enlarge and transfer (page 159) the design opposite. For the center section, follow instructions given for overlaid appliqué (page 124). Work in the following order: sky and sea behind the figures of Leda and the swan, Leda's hair, Leda's face and body, swan's body, swan's beak, Leda's arm and curl of hair, and wave in foreground. (Leave wing until last.)

(2) Piece inner border with narrow strips. Appliqué this band to overlap slightly the edge of the central panel (do not include turnbacks). Apply a narrow strip of fabric on top of the raw edges, blindstitching it in place.

(3) Piece sun's rays by machine. Overlap pre-worked sun face on top of rays and hand appliqué.

(4) To apply outside border, first stitch bottom border to the central panel, then attach the side borders, right sides facing.

(5) Stitch three layers of the wing in position. Embroider details.

An interesting alternative method of working this pattern is to enlarge the design opposite; then transfer the entire design to the reverse side of a muslin backing, drawing sun and center sections in detail, but only outlining the borders. Baste the first appliqué piece (the sky behind the figure of Leda) on the front side of the muslin. With regular machine stitching, outline around the area on the reverse side of the muslin. Turn to the right side, and trim away extra fabric close to the machine lines. Now baste in position a square of fabric for the hair. On the reverse side, outline the shape; turn to the front and again trim away the excess. Secure the edges with a zigzag stitch worked on the front. Continue, working layer by layer in this way, until you reach the final piece. Add embroidery details, such as facial features and the swan's feathers, last.

Finishing: Bring the lining over the front for a narrow binding.

Assembly chart; quilting pattern is indicated by broken lines.

FRENCH BOUQUET

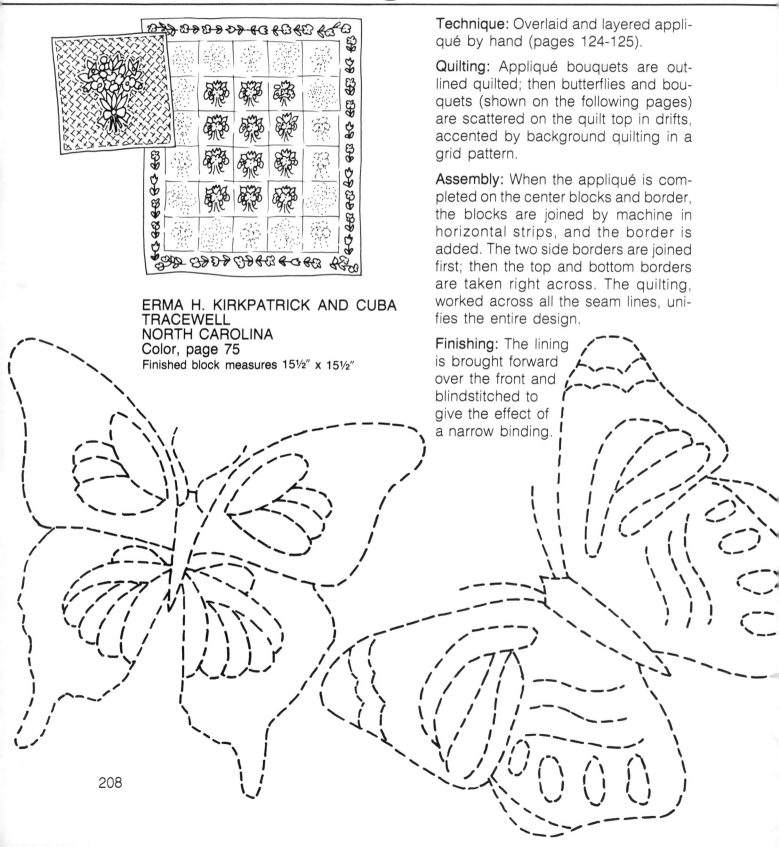

ERMA H. KIRKPATRICK AND CUBA TRACEWELL
NORTH CAROLINA
Color, page 75
Finished block measures 15½" x 15½"

Technique: Overlaid and layered appliqué by hand (pages 124-125).

Quilting: Appliqué bouquets are outlined quilted; then butterflies and bouquets (shown on the following pages) are scattered on the quilt top in drifts, accented by background quilting in a grid pattern.

Assembly: When the appliqué is completed on the center blocks and border, the blocks are joined by machine in horizontal strips, and the border is added. The two side borders are joined first; then the top and bottom borders are taken right across. The quilting, worked across all the seam lines, unifies the entire design.

Finishing: The lining is brought forward over the front and blindstitched to give the effect of a narrow binding.

Quilting patterns; actual size

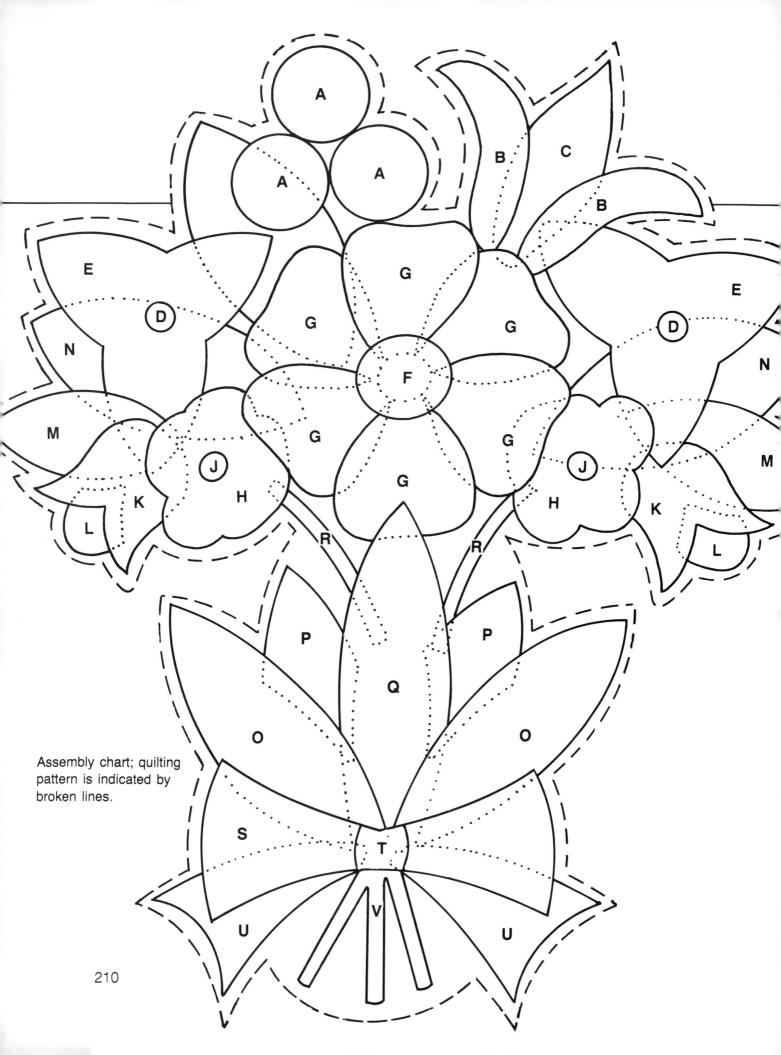

Assembly chart; quilting
pattern is indicated by
broken lines.

Pattern pieces are actual size.
Grain lines vary; cut so that the grain lines on all pieces run parallel to background fabric.

211

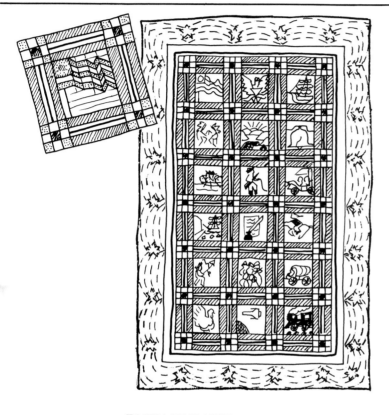

**RUTH WALKER
OKLAHOMA
Color, page 87**
Each square measures 1½" x 1½" to make a
block 12" x 12"

Technique: Machine piecing. Embroidery for details.

Quilting: Outline quilting following seams; star and swag design for border, shown opposite.

Assembly: Following the graphs on the next three pages (three are shown in color on the half-title page), cut and assemble each small square. When areas of one color are fairly large (such as the train), you can cut two squares together to form a rectangle. When half a square is needed for the effect of the design, cut a triangle. Join the squares in strips; then join the strips together to form one block.

Add embroidery touches in appropriate colors. (They are shown in black lines on the chart on the following pages.) Stem stitch, satin stitch and French knots are used most often (pages 142-143, 145).

Finishing: Piece the sashing, then join three squares across with vertical sashing in between. Join the rows together with horizontal sashing running to the edge of the row. Beyond the sashing, run a wide border with quilting, as noted above. Finish the edges with a narrow bias binding.

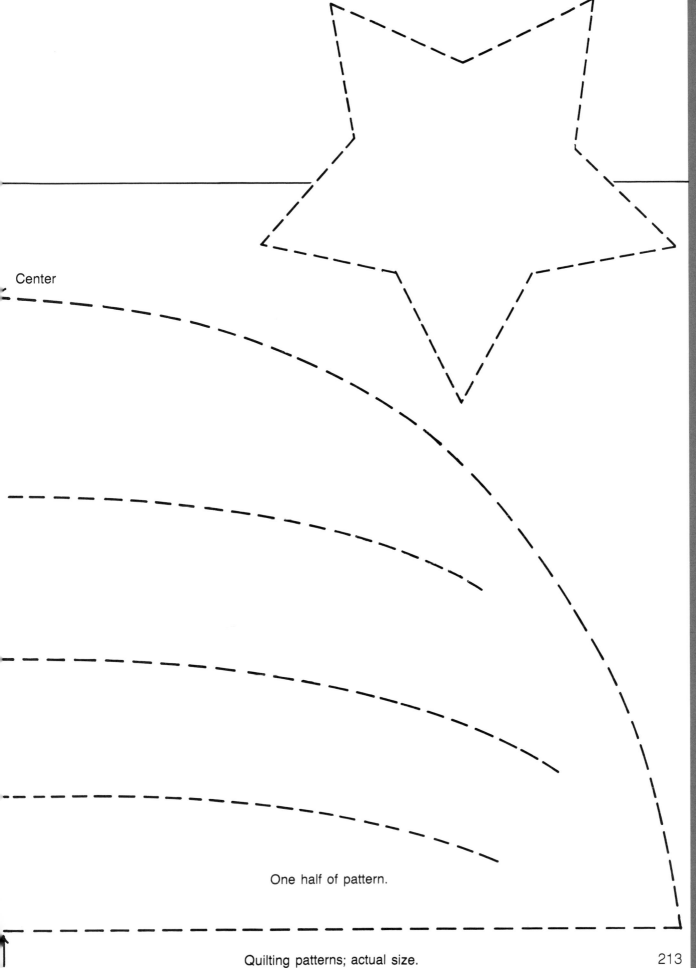

Center

One half of pattern.

Quilting patterns; actual size.

214

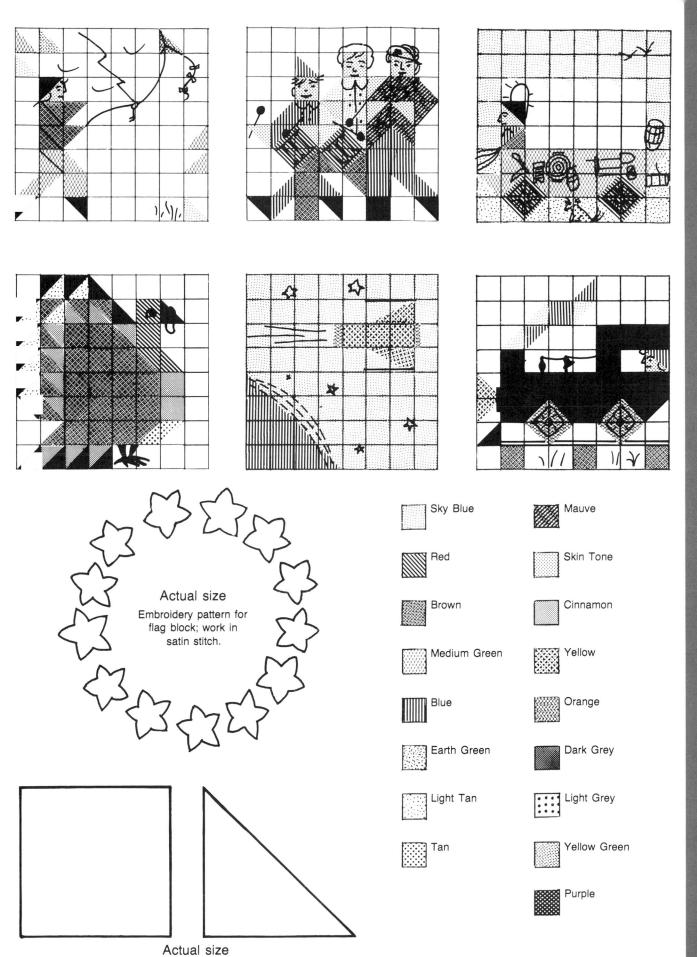

Actual size

Embroidery pattern for flag block; work in satin stitch.

Actual size

Sky Blue	Mauve
Red	Skin Tone
Brown	Cinnamon
Medium Green	Yellow
Blue	Orange
Earth Green	Dark Grey
Light Tan	Light Grey
Tan	Yellow Green
	Purple

SUPPLIERS

Pre-cut templates for
patchwork

Hearthside Crafts
P.O. Box 9120
Station E
Edmonton, Alberta T5P 4K2 Canada

Quadrille paper—large
scale graph paper

Sam Flax
55 East 55th Street
New York, NY 10022

Clear plastic suitable for
cutting templates (20
point acetate)

Charrette
212 East 54th Street
New York, NY 10022

Trace-Erase marker
Quilting frames
Leather quilter's thimble

Erica Wilson Needle Works
717 Madison Avenue
New York, NY 10021

Batting

Mountain Mist
The Stearns & Foster Co.
Cincinnati, OH 45215

"Steamstress" pressing
iron

Singer Co.
The Promenade
Rockefeller Plaza
New York, NY 10020

"Today" pressing iron

Sunbeam Appliance Co.
2001 South York Road
Oak Brook, IL 60521

Photo-sensitizing emulsion

Ace Scientific Supply Co.
P.O. Box 127
Linden, NJ 07036

D.Y.E. Textile Resources
3763 Durango Avenue
Los Angeles, CA 90034

For printing in colors

Light Impressions, Inc.
Box 3012
Rochester, NY 14614

Fiber dye companies

Fabdec
3553 Old Post Road
San Angelo, TX 76901

Pylan Products
95-10 218 Street
Queens Village, NY 11429

Pentel wax crayons

Arthur Brown Art Supply
2 West 46th Street
New York, NY 10036

Liquid embroidery

Tri-Chem Co.
Belleville, NJ 07109

Lee Wards
1200 St. Charles Street
Elgin, IL 60120

BIBLIOGRAPHY

Better Homes & Gardens Books Editors. *Better Homes & Gardens Appliqué.* Des Moines: Meredith Corp., 1978.

Beyer, Jinny. *Patchwork Patterns.* McLean, VA: EPM Publications, 1979.

Cockrell, Susan Lewis. *Anecdotes of Bessie Lewis's Quilts.* (Mrs. Fulton Lewis I).

Cooper, Patricia, and Buferd, Norma Bradley. *The Quilters: Women and Domestic Art.* Garden City, NY: Doubleday & Co., 1977.

DeGraw, Imelda G., *The Denver Art Museum: Quilts and Coverlets.* Denver: Denver Art Museum, 1974.

Fitzrandolph, Mavis. *Traditional Quilting.* London: B.T. Batsford, 1954.

Frager, Dorothy. *The Quilting Primer.* Radnor, PA: Chilton Book Co., 1974.

Haders, Phyllis. *Sunshine and Shadow: The Amish and Their Quilts.* Anaheim, CA: Main Street Press, 1976.

Ickis, Marguerite. *The Standard Book of Quilt Making and Collecting.* New York: Dover Publications, 1959.

Johnson, Bruce; Conner, Susan S.; Rogers, Josephine; and Sidford, Holly. *A Child's Comfort: Baby and Doll Quilts in American Folk Art.* New York: Harcourt Brace Jovanovich, 1977.

Johnson, Mary Elizabeth. *Prize Country Quilts.* Birmingham: Oxmoor House, 1977.

Laury, Jean Ray. *Quilts and Coverlets.* New York: Van Nostrand Reinhold Co., 1970.

McKim, Ruby S. *One Hundred & One Patchwork Patterns.* New York: Dover Publications, 1962.

Notes on Applied Work and Patchwork. London: Victoria and Albert Museum, 1949.

Notes on Quilting. London: Victoria and Albert Museum, 1949.

Orlofsky, Patsy, and Orlofsky, Myron. *Quilts in America.* New York: McGraw-Hill Book Company, 1974.

Safford, Carleton L., and Bishop, Robert. *America's Quilts and Coverlets.* New York: Barre Publishing Co., Weathervane Books, 1974.

Swan, Susan Burrows. *Plain & Fancy: American Women and Their Needlework 1700-1850.* New York: Holt, Rinehart and Winston, 1977.

INDEX

WINNERS